Tomorrow Never Waits

Tomorrow Never Waits

my life story – so far

Richard Madeley

Matador
Unit E2 Airfield Business Park,
Harrison Road, Market Harborough,
Leicestershire. LE16 7UL
Tel: 0116 2792299
Email: books@troubador.co.uk
Web: www.troubador.co.uk/matador
Twitter: @matadorbooks

ISBN 978 1805142 201

British Library Cataloguing in Publication Data.
A catalogue record for this book is available from the British Library.

Printed and bound by CPI Group (UK) Ltd, Croydon, CR0 4YY
Typeset in 11pt Minion Pro by Troubador Publishing Ltd, Leicester, UK

Matador is an imprint of Troubador Publishing Ltd

MIX
Paper | Supporting
responsible forestry
FSC
www.fsc.org FSC® C013604

Dedication

This book is dedicated to my darling wife Carol who has witnessed, endured and been roped (generally reluctantly) into multiple scrapes over the last 35 years on my behalf. She has provided sanity, perspective and quiet common sense, at times when I might have lost all three, and is the cornerstone of both my own life and the family. Darling – Thank you for everything.

Acknowledgements

I am indebted to my sister, Susan Grenfell, for her diligence, perseverance, and stamina in reading multiple versions of this book and for her valiant attempts to remind me of what I was really like as a child! Her editing was extremely valuable and a chance to reflect on many happy times together. Thank you for all your help.

Contents

Foreword

I have toyed with the idea of writing a book for many years, but have normally convinced myself that it would be a bit self-indulgent. However, reflecting on how quickly life passes, it seems that a book might be a sensible way to try and pass on some of the 'wisdom' that has found its way into my life and distil what I might otherwise have wanted to share with you in small doses over the years ahead.

Having spent most of my life being active, I have always taken physical health for granted, albeit I have broken enough bones to last a lifetime and I pray for no more accidents. But at least bones mend quickly. It is the 'plumbing and wiring' I have always rather taken for granted. As I grow older, I realise that health or misfortune can suddenly lead to a dramatic change in direction and such events seem so random and unfair that it can distract us from the fragility of our actual existence. A case in point being the tragic death of our dear friend, Friedrich Württemberg, in a car accident in May 2018. The void left by his death has focused all our thoughts.

But life has actually been very good to me and I have much

to be grateful for. This book will try and reorder some of the main themes in my life and perhaps make sense of some of the funny, silly, sad, proud and memorable moments. We all think of ourselves as special and indeed we are, although I now accept that I did not win an MC or become a general; was not a scion of the City, industry or parliament; and will probably not be knighted after all. In fact, something of a failure all round, I can hear people cry! But actually, I have had a very full and enjoyable life and one which, on reflection, would perhaps be rather difficult to lead nowadays. I was part of that post-war generation who enjoyed the last true years of innocence and this, reinforced with a very tight family upbringing, has certainly shaped my life, my values and the inner drive and competitiveness that has kept me going ever since.

This book is for my wonderful family. To thank them for their love, patience and forgiveness, for their competitiveness, encouragement and ambition, and for everything that has enriched our lives together. To Carol, Victoria, Alexandra and Robert, this is for you.

Part I

Growing Up

Chapter One

Childhood

Churches have a special smell about them. It is a combination of the musty wood of old pews and floorboards, together with candles and the lingering smell of mothballs from someone's Sunday coat. They are normally either freezing, with useless but ornate heating grills everywhere, into which I would inevitably drop my collection money, marbles or sweets, or boiling, where the back of bare legs would be scorched by some newly installed pew radiator running at 100 degrees centigrade. We seemed to spend a lot of time in church as children and my memories of looking at Dad's shoes and socks as he prayed are still fresh in my mind, even now. In fact, I recall sitting with my own son, Robert, many years later in the school chapel at Horris Hill wondering if he was thinking the same!

Both Mum and Dad were the offspring of parents who held deeply Christian and devout views. Dad's parents met in France during WWI where his mother, Violet Pixley, was a nurse. She lost both her brothers in the war, including Reggie, my namesake, who won an MC in the Royal Flying Corps before being shot down in 1916. Violet, distraught at the loss of her brothers, became devoted to Dick, Dad's father, who, as a conscientious objector, drove ambulances in France during the war. He, too, had developed a somewhat puritanical form of worship and, accordingly, Dad was brought up in their rather intense and serious home. I remember Grandfather as being quite reserved and often rather dour, although we saw a fun side to him when he was dispensing black treacle or hot orange juice – a rather odd beverage he enjoyed at elevenses. He was also good at sleight of hand and managed to convince me that he could thread a walnut from one ear, right through his head and out of the other ear. Needless to say, I ended up with very sore ears trying to copy him. Granny, by comparison, was an absolute treasure in every respect and had a sort of timeless Victorian quality about her. She used to join us camping every year until well into her eighties. I was about thirteen when Grandfather died and I remember being amused by his Alzheimer's, which in his case resulted in him locking everything he could find and then pocketing the key. Dad and Granny spent ages trying to match up keys and locks after he died, but several doors and box lids had to be sawn open!

Mum was the youngest of six, born to missionaries in Africa and much of her early life was spent in Africa where her father, Harold Guillebaud, ran one of the early missionary stations in Rwanda and Burundi. Although she came back to school in England, her abiding childhood memories are of Africa and, undoubtedly, this was her spiritual home. It was also clear that she harboured hopes of following in her father's footsteps, as had four of her older siblings, and she was deeply upset when these plans foundered. Her father died very young, during the war, and her plans unravelled in the early post-war period of uncertainty. Her mother, Margaret (née Edwards, the cousin of the well-known painter Lionel Edwards), lived on in Cambridge and one of my only memories of her is of being scolded for pulling the tail of her cat, Mwami, and getting scratched for my efforts. Granny (Guillebaud) was a prolific and very good artist and we still enjoy many of her pictures around our houses. I wish I had stronger memories of her, but I just recall a big dark house and not being allowed to touch anything. Enough about grandparents!

I was born on Tuesday 22nd January 1957 at about 3.30am, at Agars Plough – our rather oddly named home in Lower Kingswood, just outside Reigate in Surrey. Agars Plough is, in fact, the name of one of the playing fields at Eton, which Dad thought resembled the view from the back of the house across the fields. A home birth is more unusual now, but I am rather pleased to have arrived directly into the family home without a lot of the rigmarole that seems to accompany hospital births these days. The attendant family doctor was Dr Dick, a wonderfully old-fashioned GP, who came to the house with his big doctor's bag and dispensed common sense and/or aspirin for almost everything. He was the first of many doctors I have grown to know over my life.

Agars Plough was a magical home down the end of a long country lane, Margery Lane, on Colley Hill, now a little too close to the M25 for my liking, but back then it was rural tranquillity at its best. The house was set in about two acres with a small wood at one end, and the garden and lawns unfolding behind the house down to a separate 'lower' garage where Dad used to keep his old Douglas motorbike and the camping trailer. The house was a curious architectural mixture of styles with a large former artist's studio at one end, half of which had been converted into our drawing room and the other half being the main garage. The rest of the house was a maze of rooms, stairs, landings and an attic where we would hide away when we'd been naughty.

Given my parents' upbringing, you might be excused for thinking that my childhood must have been puritanical, unloving and rather dysfunctional, but it wasn't. In fact, Susan (eighteen months older), Mark (twenty months younger) and I enjoyed a loving, sheltered and close family upbringing, which instilled in each of us a strong sense of family identity that we have taken with us through life. However, though we didn't realise it at the time, our life was very insular and we lived in a rather introspective bubble. Neither of our parents had enjoyed what would be regarded now as a normal, socially active upbringing and so their sense of normal was a more formal and structured life where we created our own entertainment. I think I was seven when we got our first TV and it was a special treat to be able to watch Trooping the Colour (in black and white) or *The Black and White Minstrel Show*, a dance show that would now be regarded as horribly racist. TV was also forbidden on Sundays. It was an old-fashioned upbringing in many respects where we had time to embrace old-fashioned values, reinforced by our weekly trips to church and Bible study. Given the pace of social change taking place around us in the late fifties and the 'Swinging Sixties', with its sex, drugs and rock 'n' roll, perhaps this was Mum and Dad's way of trying to protect us and create routine, certainty and security. In our innocence, we, of course, didn't question things and so we happily enjoyed our close-knit family life, without knowing too much about the big bad world out there – a situation that is almost impossible to imagine in today's febrile world of social media and instant gratification.

Margery Lane was a dead end so had little passing traffic and Sue and I used to invent our own stories and play-act our adventures around the garden or house. Dad had inherited an old Gipsy caravan from his parents, which was parked in the trees close to the house, and we loved playing 'happy families' there, reluctantly including Mark when he was bigger, and generally living in our imaginary world. We called it Pooh Corner and it was a wonderful escape for us all. There was a convenient branch on which we could swing from the back platform of the caravan and this gave us hours of amusement and spectacular falls. Across the lane from the caravan was a small convenience store, Miss Tingley's, where sweets of all descriptions could be bought individually from big glass jars for only a few pence (old money). Most of our pocket money was spent there.

Compared to today, life was very relaxed and trust was both given and expected. Mum would normally drive us to school in the morning, but most evenings we would catch the number 406 bus back up to Margery Lane and walk up the lane home. Considering Sue and I were both under seven, this was enormous freedom, but we just thought it was perfectly normal. On one occasion, she and I decided to walk home from school up Reigate Hill (just over two miles) to save the bus fare. We must have looked abandoned as a coal lorry stopped and picked us up and drove us home, where the driver then scolded Mum for having allowed us to try and walk this distance alone. She had no idea that we had chosen to do so to save a few pence for sweets in Miss Tingley's and we got into terrible trouble for our pains! Sometimes, we would miss our bus anyway by watching the steam trains coming into Reigate Station, which was at the end of the road from our pre-prep school, Micklefield. Although most of the steam trains were being replaced by diesels in the 1950s, there were still a few in regular operation and it was always fun watching them at the level crossing, puffing and steaming through town, with their high-pitched whistles frightening the unsuspecting.

Among the happiest memories from childhood were our annual camping trips. We didn't know it at the time, but we assumed that Mum and Dad loved camping – and to some extent, they did. However, it was largely from financial necessity (to keep costs down) that each year we would spend two to three weeks under canvas in different parts of the country. Camping is, of course, an adventure and I still love it, having done it professionally for a number of years when I was in the Royal Marines. The adventure would start when the ancient camping trailer was wheeled around from the lower garage and stocked up with our food and equipment. The trailer was the most extraordinary-looking vehicle, which Dad had converted with large sheets of hardboard and Perspex to create a living space around a fixed central table. Most bizarrely of all, he had painted the outside a very conspicuous salmon pink colour with paint left over from the redecoration of the house. In fact, I was never sure why he painted the house pink either, but the trailer was certainly a head-turner wherever we went and, frankly, an eyesore when we arrived in some beautiful remote field and set up camp. But we only thought of it as individual and distinctive, rather than simply odd – which, of course, it was! Perhaps for this reason I have always opted for small green or camouflaged tents ever since.

Part of the camping adventure was having Granny (Pixley) with us. Grandfather never came camping as he didn't really enjoy travelling away from home, but Granny's presence was a joy and her wonderfully Victorian clothes, beach attire, general demeanour and her unique old people's smell made her such a special part of our lives. Those early seaside holidays were memorable and wonderfully innocent. Sandcastles in the shape of cars or working volcanoes (a hollowed-out sandcastle in which we would set fire to some driftwood) were some of our specialities, along with exploring caves, catching crabs (which Mark seemed to like) and burying Dad. Latterly, and rather to Mum's frustration, we began to go on touring holidays rather than staying put in one place. Mum always found such trips exhausting, but gamely supported Dad's itchy feet and a restlessness I can now sometimes recognise in myself.

Christmas was another magical memory of childhood, together with the genuine belief that an old man with a beard, dressed in red, actually delivered presents. The overwhelming excitement of Christmas is easy to recall and one of life's great joys as a parent. Christmas, for us, was normally spent in Chertsey with Granny and Grandfather and, after they had died, in Cambridge with my Aunt Mary's family, the Stockleys, or at our house. Dad was the mystical man, walking up the garden on Christmas Day dressed in a red coat and wearing a rather scary mask and beard. As with children over the generations, we were swept away with the story and didn't challenge the obvious. I vividly recall the shock and sadness when my cousin broke the news to me, aged seven, that it was all a hoax – I couldn't and didn't want to accept it. How wonderful it was for me, years later, to see Alexandra still enthralled by the myth aged twelve and our concern that we should break the news to her before she went to Downe House, lest she be teased!

The Stockley cousins were, in fact, our main external group of friends and very special they were to us, too. Tom, Aunt Mary's husband, died of a heart attack in his early forties, placing a huge strain on the family and Mary, in particular. The five children had a difficult start and we felt extraordinarily lucky by comparison. I spent a lot of time with them in Cambridge before joining the Royal Marines and Philip, the closest to me in age, became a great companion as we rebuilt motorbikes and generally misbehaved. Mary was later to play a big mentoring role for me as I faced separation and divorce from my first wife, Debbie, and was a huge help to me in those dark days – but more of that later.

Adolescence is never a particularly attractive or enjoyable phase in life and mine was no different. The butt of my frustrations was normally poor Mark, whose only misfortune was to be different from me and less interested in the things I wanted to do. In my defence, he also had a knack of goading me into action, then ensuring I always got caught red-handed at the critical moment! I have few memories of getting into trouble with him at Agar's Plough, but after we moved to our next home in North Derbyshire, Bridge House, we certainly managed to test a few lows.

Probably the worst was when I shot him with my air rifle. We had decided, one day, to take some of our old Airfix models down to the sunken garden, a reasonably safe area that Dad had approved as our .22 range. We set the models up and began blasting away until the turn came to shoot a splendid model of the Queen Mary liner I had made. I naturally wanted the first shot, but Mark decided it was his turn, which, of course, it may well have been, but I didn't see why small details like that should spoil my fun. He went and sat next to the ship and refused to move, thereby assuming I wouldn't shoot. Wrong! The ensuing shot was rather bad luck as it hit something behind the model and the pellet ricocheted, hit him on the knee and then the side of his face, right next to his eye. It was probably more from surprise than actual hurt that he screamed blue murder. Concerned only with the prospect of having my rifle confiscated, the loss of pocket money and other privileges, I concluded that the only way to stop him crying and ensure he didn't tell Mum and Dad was the threat of even worse violence. To my surprise, this worked, which probably says something rather dark about my relationship with him at that time, but to his credit he stood by his word and never did tell on me, although he certainly got his own back in different ways.

His first reprisal was a few days later when he climbed into my tree house (he had one in another tree) and threw all the contents down. Actually, this didn't amount to a huge quantity of anything, but was a nuisance and required several trips up the rope ladder. It was the discovery of this incident that was amusing; Sue and I were cycling fast down the path running alongside the trees, when I saw the pile of wood etc. lying beneath my tree house. I slammed on my brakes and said, "Look what Mark has done!" Poor Sue didn't have time to look – or do anything else, for that matter – as she crashed into the back of my stationary bicycle and I recall seeing her strangely crouching shape as she flew over my head to land in a heap several yards away. Fortunately, she wasn't hurt and it remains one of our funniest memories from that time.

Life at home during the school holidays became a bit more manageable for me (and certainly for Mum) when Mark moved into his own bedroom in the part of the house vacated by grandparents after they died. Not having to start every day with a fight was a blessing. One of our favourite pastimes was dressing up and we three children were often charging around the garden with me dressed in Dad's old WWII battledress, Mark wearing Grandfather's old Special Constable hat and Sue looking like Florence Nightingale with something she found deep in the dressing-up box. It was pure innocence and make-believe with a plot that normally involved Mark as the casualty being nursed back to life by Sue. It never occurred to us that it might be considered somewhat childish until we bumped into some young boys, trespassing at the bottom of our garden, who teased us mercilessly.

What we all missed as children were like-minded friends during the holidays. We all had our school friends, but living in north Derbyshire meant that we hardly saw anyone our age outside term time. We had virtually no local friends to speak of and those very few families who lived within cycling distance also seemed a little odd to us. It was probably even worse for Sue, who, being the oldest, must have gone stir-crazy living with two juvenile, warring brothers. She also made it clear pretty quickly that she didn't like me using her for rugby tackling practice! But Sue and I were (and still are) on the same wavelength, have the same cranky sense of humour and sense of the ridiculous. We would spend ages sitting together after term ended, catching up on news, scandal, gossip and all the normal trivialities that engross adolescents. However, it was a huge relief all round when we moved south to Beaconsfield, via Cambridge, for a few months in 1973 and the last few years of childhood were spent in a rather more sociable environment, which was an eye-opener and conveniently coincided with my senior years at Eton.

The move south also overlapped with my introduction to motorbikes. Just before leaving Bridge House, Dad and I had bought and rebuilt an old 150cc James two-stroke motorbike. It cost £3 from a local scrapyard! The excitement (and surprise) when it fired into life as I was pushed down the main lawn was incredible and gave me that instant taste of independence, a taste that has lasted ever since. Having mastered riding it around the fields and tested several conventional and less conventional dismounts, I realised that motorbikes equalled freedom. As soon as I turned sixteen, I was legally allowed to ride a motorbike under 250cc and immediately went and bought an old British Francis Barnett 250cc, which I repainted and smartened up and then drove all around the Chilterns. It was the most wonderful escape from the confines of home, although there were a number of very close shaves as I rode with my chin on the tank trying to get the speedo over 65mph. I traded the 'Franny B' for a Triumph Tiger Cub 200cc trials bike the following year and this was possibly the best bike I ever owned. It was light, had knobbly trail tyres and a low ratio sprocket, which meant I could (and did) go everywhere. What fun! I also discovered that I preferred balance and riding skill over speed, which was probably a mercy.

There comes a moment in all children's lives when they realise, normally with some disappointment, that their parents aren't actually as cool, clever, kind or helpful as we had expected... or needed. I'm not talking about the ability of parents to embarrass their children, which seems to be a natural talent passed down from one generation to the next without any trouble. Dancing, dress sense and technological incompetence being obvious examples. No, I mean where children actually need guidance and a role model to follow in dealing with important moments or decisions in their lives. I felt it as a parent years later when Victoria challenged me on something important and it upset me greatly to know that I had failed to live up to her expectations.

Dad was naturally quite a shy, reticent man and I suspect he struggled in the cut and thrust of commerce despite his instinctive acumen. Perhaps he was too kind. His career fell into three phases; the first being war-time service, where he seems to have enjoyed a varied and exciting time building roads and airstrips in Burma, riding motorcycles around and generally overseeing more major construction projects than most engineers do in a lifetime. The second phase was in engineering and marketing roles at BOC, Unilever and Doncaster's – a steel foundry in Sheffield (hence our move up north), where his company produced precision (drop) forged turbine blades among other things. Mum famously referred to them as forge droppings (instead of drop forgings), instantly blowing her credibility, much to Dad's embarrassment. The last phase was possibly his most fulfilling, namely as head of the St John's charitable organisation in London. But I sensed that Dad was not overly ambitious and as such had a different outlook on life and how to motivate us children. As much as I loved him and enjoyed all the things we did together, I regret that he never really helped me at the critical times I needed to make decisions, whether at school or, indeed, in my career. As such, although he commented and gave useful feedback after the fact, most of the key decisions were largely mine alone. Mum, by contrast, was ambitious, having a youngest child's inferiority complex that made her fight for everything. Undoubtedly, I owe my tenacity to her. But she had never had a career beyond her short war-time role in the WAAF, working on radios and electronic circuitry. As such, she had a somewhat homespun view on life, laced with reflected wisdom, which she aired at every chance to legitimise her views. Unfortunately, this tendency led me to generally disregard a lot of what she said and I dare say I missed a lot of valuable advice along with the guff and narrow-mindedness that accompanied it.

Such reflections shape slowly in a child and certainly these thoughts have matured over time and probably read more harshly than is entirely fair. Indeed, Sue, Mark and I remain remarkably close on an emotional and family level, even if our lives have diverged as our careers and lives have developed. But despite the love and closeness of our family, which remains an abiding memory, there was an underlying frustration that we lived in a cocoon, not properly prepared for the wider world and with a charming innocence that maybe wasn't necessarily either charming or helpful in today's world. As I realised later, bringing up children is not easy and many parents struggle to relinquish the simplicity and unquestioned love of early childhood, and then fail to adapt to changing demands and needs as each child grows up and develops their own identity and interests. I hope this is not how Carol and I will be judged by Victoria, Alexandra and Robert! But more about parenting in due course, as long before children arrived, I still had plenty of childhood and growing up to do myself.

I have deliberately separated my childhood memories into those at home and those at school, on which I will focus in the next chapter, as there are always two different personas that exist in each of us: our private family lives and our public, outward characters. I have often thought that school life and the advent of peer pressure, external influence and puberty all conspire to supress the real character and drivers in us, and that this slowly re-emerges somewhere in one's mid-twenties. The real nature, spirit, drive and longer-term potential of a boy (and I can only really comment about us chaps) is often visible in its unvarnished and somewhat raw state aged seven. I think that I have struggled to rediscover that magic age ever since, but I look back at that person and see many characteristics that have lived with me ever since, and I know my children still accuse me of being a *Peter Pan* character. But, for me, the next test of childhood was about to unfold – school.

With my mother and Susan – 1957

*Running through the dunes on holiday in something my
mother knitted for me!*

Looking poised and elegant, aged 3

Relaxing at Agars Plough

With Susan and my father at Agars Plough

Camping with Granny and the trailer and the Morris Minor

Susan, my mother, me and Granny in the background

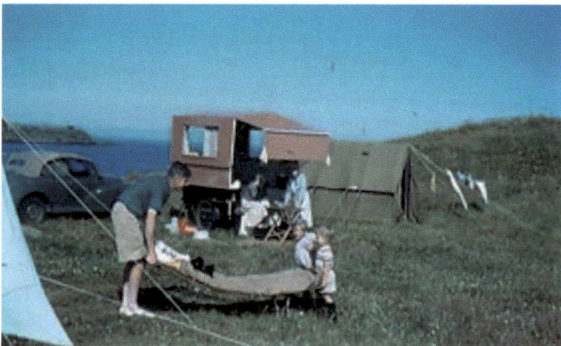

Helping my father move beds

With Mark on my first motorbike, in the orchard at Bridge House

A view of Bridge House from the garden

On my Triumph Tiger Cub at our home in Beaconsfield – 1974

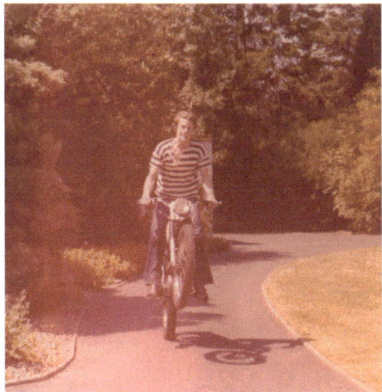

Chapter Two

School

Marlborough House School in Hawkhurst, Kent was a typical boys-only preparatory school of the time. It was spartan by modern standards and, on reflection, the teachers were a rather strange lot with names like Major Pardoe (carpentry), Mr Briggs (English), Miss Creswell (for first-year boys – she was a sweetie), Miss Lawrence (matron and effectively 'mother' to 105 boys) and in charge of them all was Geoff Martin, a wonderful big man with a deep, booming voice, an MC from the war and a wooden leg to prove it. I simply loved the place.

I arrived at MHS, as we called it, in September 1964, aged seven and a half, in my short trousers, even shorter haircut and wide eyes. I remember to this day the feeling of total abandonment when Mum and Dad drove out of the gates in their old green Hillman car, leaving me behind with a bunch of other teary-eyed boys all struggling to contain their emotions. It seems almost impossibly barbaric in these days of mobile phones, cuddly toys, duvets, etc. that we would not see our families again for six weeks at half term – in the shorter Lent terms of only ten weeks, there was no exeat at all!

Our dormitory was called 'Stowe' after the public school, as were the names of the various other dormitories in the main house, 'Winchester', 'Malvern', 'Bryanston', etc. For some reason, there was no 'Eton' or 'Harrow', which I discovered later was because Geoff Martin disliked them. There were six iron beds in Stowe, each made up with hospital corners, giving the room a very functional feel with bare floorboards and a rather plain ceiling light. There was no central heating, although our dormitory was, in fact, the only one with running water, with a small sink behind a door in the corner. The other dormitories all used enamel basins for morning and evening washes, and we otherwise all shared a large communal bathroom for our biweekly baths.

I felt completely unprepared for school, despite having attended Micklefield pre-prep in Reigate for a couple of years. All I recall there was of pretending to be an aeroplane in the school recreation ground, frightening everyone in my way and painting dinosaurs in art. No one had really told me what school was for or what was expected of me. The result was that I decided that school was an adventure, interspersed with some boring lessons about the three Rs. At least I was top of the class in divinity, which seemed a doddle after all the indoctrination at home, but generally I was not a natural student. By contrast, I found my natural habitat on the sports fields and this was a key part of life at MHS, with the headmaster championing all of us to 'do our best and make him proud'. I also discovered that outside of sports and class, there was ample scope for adventure and play and, providing you didn't get caught, you could do almost anything. I found myself rising to this challenge, even if I did end up getting caught more than I would have liked!

The school building dated from the late nineteenth century and was a substantial house laid out over three main floors. Over the years it had grown with additional buildings, such as the changing rooms and shower complex, with junior classrooms above, linked by a cold glazed corridor. Most of the ground-floor rooms of the main school were classrooms, but there was also a row of purpose-built classrooms constructed by the school's in-house builder, Bubbles. Bubbles was an amazing character, although I dare say he would have struggled with today's building regulations. However, he was always cheery to us boys and had clearly enjoyed a full life. The school was set in about fifty acres of land with a separate and large gymnasium, three main sports pitches, a swimming pool and a chapel. It also had a large area below the main playing fields with two large ponds and a wooded dell, where we could build tree houses and set up camps. In the pre-health and safety world, we built some elaborate tree houses – some dangerously high and wobbly. It is amazing we never had any serious accidents. I preferred making underground hideouts with lots of camouflage and secret entrances from which to surprise passing marauders. Others played in the mud at the bottom of the dell, creating dams, ponds and all sorts of weird water shoots.

Organisationally, the school was split into four teams of about twenty-six boys: Audrey, Dunbar, Egan and Hawkins. I was in Dunbar, which then became my tribal team for everything from sports to behaviour, academic achievement and general deportment. There was a 'Good Citizenship Board', which had every boy's name listed and a variety of categories against which 'red' and/or 'black' marks were made. A red mark scored +2 points and a black mark was -1 point. The totals were tallied up at the end of each term to see which individual was the supreme 'goody-goody' and which team had won overall. Contrary to family myth, I was quite a 'good citizen' most of the time and I also benefitted from the patronage of the headmaster, who liked my pluck and my generally uninhibited approach to life. He called me 'Midge' because of my diminutive size and, undoubtedly, sowed the seeds of a military career in my mind with his encouragement to be a leader, not a follower, and leading by example in all walks of life.

School time sometimes seemed interminable, with subjects like Latin creating new challenges. I think the high point in my life's accomplishment of Latin was achieved aged eight and a half when I scored ninety-four per cent in the end of term exams. It was a steady downhill slide thereafter, although sadly I had to carry on studying it for a further seven years. However, I enjoyed much of the curriculum and made steady, if unspectacular, progress. It was also reassuring to find that there were plenty of boys who found it much harder than me and, as I discovered during my Royal Marines training many years later, there is nothing more motivating than seeing someone else struggle and not wanting to be classed with them. I found that I was quite good at geometry and liked the accuracy of scale drawings and working out angles. In fact, despite my handwriting, which has become steadily worse through my life, I was very tidy and liked to be organised and structured in everything. But memories can also be funny and recently I found an old English workbook from 1968, which I had saved for some reason, and there was a priceless comment by Mr Briggs, scrawled in red at the bottom of a rather inadequate essay: 'Don't think you can get away with this, Madeley!'

Sport was what I loved and I engaged at all levels in anything I could. What I lacked in talent, I made up for in enthusiasm and energy. But in gymnastics, I found that my upper body strength enabled me to attempt more adventurous pieces of equipment and I was soon on the gym team. I loved parallel bars and the vaulting horse and earned a reputation for some spectacular vaults. Floor work was never my specialty, but I did manage the school's first ever flick flack – a backwards handspring, which probably accounts for the bad back I've had ever since. Outside the gym, athletics was obvious as I loved running and hurdling. But field sports and teamwork were what I really enjoyed. Rugby, or 'rugger' as it was more commonly known then, was my favourite as it coupled handling skills with simple out-and-out bravery. I was scrum half and determined to be the hardest tackler on the field and would never let anyone through. I still remember the praise from the headmaster when I floored a tall, lanky forward in an inter-school match, two yards from the try line, with only two minutes to go. We won! My fly half partner and great friend was David Gower, and he and I made an inseparable team.

David rapidly became my 'best friend' at school and since he lived in Loughborough, which was only an hour from Bridge House in North Derbyshire, we occasionally met up during the school holidays. David was unbelievably gifted and excelled at everything, both in the classroom and in sports, and he went on to play cricket and subsequently captain the England team. He had a strong positive influence on those around him and, undoubtedly, got me to focus more constructively on my studies than perhaps might otherwise have been the case. But our friendship didn't start well. David arrived at MHS a year after me and had the misfortune to have been sent to school with pink pyjamas. How his mother could have packed these and not questioned their suitability in a single sex boys' school escaped me. Hardened after a year at the school and with battle scars from numerous dormitory raids to show for it, I took it upon myself to 'sort him out'. His bed was next to mine and one night I decided that I would toughen him up. With sheet change the following morning, I took my bed apart and put a sheet over my head and pretended to be a ghost. I launched myself off my bed at him, making a scary high-pitch roar that I thought was suitably ghost-like. Unfortunately, I misjudged the distance between our beds and my shin hit the cast-iron frame of his bed, whereupon my roar turned into a scream of agony. By this time, I was right on top of him and he woke up in a panic and started screaming in genuine fear. Needless to say, the lights went on a few moments later and in walked the matron, headmaster and half the neighbouring dormitory. I recall that was about the fifth time I was beaten.

Pretending to be a ghost must have been a theme at the time, as I can remember another occasion in that same dormitory when I decided to try and scare everyone. I got to the room ahead of the other boys for our after-lunch rest (we all had to read our books for half an hour before heading out for sports) and decided to climb up inside the old chimney, which behind the washstands on one wall. Being as small as I was, I found I could wriggle my way out of sight above the entrance to the fireplace and there I waited until everyone arrived. I then started to make suitable ghost noises and had fun listening to the confusion about what it was and where it was coming from. I gradually raised the volume and thought it enormous fun as they clearly had no idea until, suddenly, fifty years' worth of soot and debris became dislodged and fell on top of me, propelling me out in a heap into the fireplace. I looked like a comic book chimney sweep, covered from head to toe in a grey sticky residue and my clothes completely ruined. Furthermore, half the dormitory was covered in a cloud of dust, which seemed to go everywhere. Once again, a trip to the headmaster ended that little escapade.

The routine of school provided a reassuring background to growing up. Mum and Dad had moved up to North Derbyshire after I had been at the school for a year and so the distance from home to school had suddenly increased from a couple of hours to a full day, making half-term visits or exeats difficult. Although I rapidly became absorbed by school activities, I always found the process of saying my goodbyes an impossibly difficult moment, whether this was at the school gates or, as more often became the case, on the school train from Charing Cross. I was puzzled why I had been the first to leave home when I was the middle child. Sue and Mark both went to day school in Sheffield for another two years while I was the only one 'cast out' at boarding school. It always made for emotional and rather contrived exeats from school, staying in guest houses in the local area rather than going home. I did on occasions stay with friends' parents and this was great fun, although not strictly 'home time' for me. Strangely, when Mark joined me at MHS, looking after him helped distract me from my own sadness and homesickness, and I know Mark suffered far worse than I did.

For all the false bravado and inevitable stresses of growing up, school was a wonderfully innocent and uncomplicated world. We worked, we had fun, we were naughty, we got punished and we moved on to run the cycle again. MHS was a world in itself, where the structure and certainty of our lives was secure and comforting. Old-fashioned concepts such as 'work hard and play hard' became our mantra, and honesty, integrity and doing our duty were ingrained into us. Geoff Martin was an inspirational headmaster, involving himself with everyone. He would oversee our letter-writing home every weekend and read us books once a week in the school hall, something which we all loved. His strange gait and the bonking noise his wooden leg would make nearly always gave us plenty of time to hide if we were being naughty, and he used to joke about holding his socks up with drawing pins. All in all, he was everyone's hero, both boys and staff, and he taught French to the senior boys when he wasn't running everything else.

As we reached the top of the school, the senior boys took on roles as dormitory captains and other leadership roles. It was also the moment when emergent hormones made us a little more aware of the pretty under matrons, normally eighteen-year-old girls doing a gap year, who were sent to help. I recall getting completely obsessed with one young girl, the sister of a fellow boy who arrived in one of my last terms, and one dangerously naughty summer afternoon with her in the back of the grass truck inside the pavilion, experimenting with kissing and misplaced groping. It seems unimaginable now and would have probably been a reportable offence even then – I was only twelve, after all!

But, sadly, my life at MHS was coming to an end. I had matured enormously (although arguably not enough) over the five years and had proven myself as a competent and brave (reckless, some may say) sportsman, an adequate student and an angelic chorister. Singing the solo of 'Once in Royal David's City' in the Hawkhurst parish church was a highlight, even if I did end the verse a semi-tone sharp! Equally, I had learned some really important lessons about myself, how to interact with others and the responsibilities of leadership. Geoff Martin had given me a clear sense of purpose and I found that having got a lot of the silly naughtiness out of my system, I now wanted to get on with being more grown-up.

Eton was a very different experience altogether and not what I expected at all. Having been one of the top boys in a small, cossetted prep school, I was now back at the bottom in a much bigger, more diverse place, where multiple emerging egos and personalities were all fighting for precedence, and where the breadth of peer group talent and traditions of the school and its facilities were on a completely different scale. I suddenly felt insecure on multiple levels. I was still only twelve and a half and one of the youngest in my year. In fact, I never understood why I wasn't in the year below with boys of my own age. I also started Eton in a different house for my first term (we called terms 'halves' just to confuse outsiders), which meant that I also lost the important early bonding with my house contemporaries. It was not a propitious start, but Dad had been at Eton, as had all his cousins and Pixley forebears, so it was clearly what had to be done and I got stuck in.

I was quickly selected for the College Chapel Special Choir, which proved to be very rewarding and meant that I would spend my entire Eton career in the main chapel rather than having to graduate from the lower chapel (with over 1,100 boys, we needed two chapels to accommodate everyone). The special choir was a useful focus for me and I loved singing. Although it necessitated two separate rehearsals per week, the quality of the choir was superb and we sang at numerous venues including King's College Chapel, Cambridge – Eton's sister chapel – where the acoustics were spectacular. I also quite enjoyed processing into chapel in our scarlet robes and surpluses after everyone else had sat down. On one occasion, I had been fiddling with the ornate carving in the pew and managed to get my finger stuck in a hole, resulting in me having to remain in my seat while the rest of the choir recessed, leaving me looking very foolish until the chapel cleared and I could finally, and painfully, extract my throbbing finger.

Daily life quickly took on its routine and the novelty of the school uniform soon passed. The school had about twenty houses, each with some fifty boys, and there was a separate college house for the scholars. The housemaster for my first half was Jack Anderson, known as 'Jack the Ripper' both for his predilection for 'ripping' poor work and also for his fiery temper. A 'rip' was a poor piece of work, where the teacher would literally tear the top of the page. This then had to be signed off by one's housemaster and tutor, who appended suitably disparaging comments. I ended up with quite a few rips over the years and probably more than the opposite form of treatment, a 'show up', which was for good work, likewise signed off by housemaster and tutor. I felt that Jack Anderson took a bit of a dislike to me and I was always in trouble. Granted, I probably deserved it and on one occasion I threw a tin of baked beans at my friend, Barney White-Spunner, cutting his head open, resulting in him having to be stitched up in the school sanatorium. Barney went on to be a major general and was knighted, but he has never let me forget the scar on his head!

After my term at JA (we abbreviated house names to the initials of the housemaster), I joined RHP, where Raymond Parry became my new nemesis. Parry, a history teacher, was a fiery Welshman with a quick temper. We learned to treat him with great respect and the house established a tight sense of identity around his feisty temperament. Fortunately, there was a trio of habitually naughty boys, Greig, Parshall and Lyall Grant, who deflected most of the heat and for that I was grateful. My year group at RHP was, by good fortune, one of the most impressive and successful of its generation and our reunions some fifty years later reflect the extraordinary diversity and success of that shaggy group of boys from 1970, even the 'naughty ones'! But the early days were not always easy and cliques quickly established, largely based on prep school affiliations, and I felt very much apart. My choir practices and the Bible study groups, which Mum insisted I attend, quickly labelled me as a goody-goody and I endured a lot of difficult teasing in the early years. This was compounded by a nagging knee injury that prevented me from playing contact sports and so, after early success in the junior teams, I was unable to establish my sporting credentials, which I regarded as half my identity. If only my studies could have compensated for this, but at Eton I was in the lower half of most classes and found the pace of learning much more demanding. Those first couple of years were very tough and the onset of puberty only seemed to make things worse.

Acting was not my forte, but each year we put on a house play and the productions in the Farrer Theatre were very impressive considering they were entirely managed by the boys themselves. At MHS, my first role was as a tree in *Robin Hood*. I remember wearing a green bodysuit and being draped in leaves, having to keep my arms up as branches. Inevitably, the arms drooped and my nose itched and I was probably the most active tree in Sherwood Forest. I did get a small speaking part as King John in *1066 and All That*, but it was clear I wasn't going to be applying to Equity any time soon. At Eton, my biggest part was as a dead body in *Billy Budd*. I fell from the rigging with a big scream and then my body was carried on. Sadly, I even 'corpsed' as a dead body so wasn't invited to act again.

With contact sports off the agenda, I returned to gymnastics, which I had enjoyed so much at prep school. My fitness was untroubled by the growing pains in my knee and I soon found that the rings, high bar and vaulting gave me plenty of outlet for my energies. I won a place on the team and then my colours, and even went on to compete in the Berkshire schools competitions. But gymnastics was deemed a minor sport at Eton, so it lacked the credibility of the main sports. However, I found that my size was an advantage as a cox and I ended up coxing various of the school eights, which was enormous fun. Furthermore, this was a major sport and so I began to earn some visibility as a 'wet bob' (a rower, as a opposed to 'dry bob', a cricketer). Watching Robert coxing at Cheltenham many years later brought back some wonderful memories of house bumping races and long summer afternoons spent on the river. Annoyingly, I started to grow at about fifteen and then ended up too big to be a cox, but not really big enough to be a credible oarsman. However, I did end up in the 4th eight (there were seven) and we raced in regattas around the country, pretending to be very serious.

Exams! A word that can still conjure cold sweats and nail biting. Eton used to have its own school exams, called Trials, at the end of each half (except Lent) – and trials they were. The main advantage of Trials, however, was that they prepared us for O and A levels and we all became familiar with working under exam conditions. Academic work at Eton involved considerable independent study and personal time management with deadlines for 'EW' (homework was known as 'Extra Work' or 'EW'), which we had to manage around our other obligations. It was a good lesson in self-discipline and time management and meant that we had considerable freedom to organise our free time. However, it did require self-motivation and while I could just about cope in most subjects, I struggled in others. I recall Mum organising some extra French and maths coaching during the holidays and this undoubtedly helped in these two subjects. But I would put them in the same category as enforced ballroom dancing lessons with spotty-faced girls and sweaty hands; necessary, but not very enjoyable.

We took O levels in two tranches: the first in year two (I was fourteen), in English language, maths, French and Latin. The remainder – English literature, history, geography, Spanish, additional maths (calculus), physics and the General Paper – followed a year later, together with Latin, which I had to retake. It sounds every bit as traumatic now as it did at the time, but I passed nine and headed on to A level study in history, geography and economics. History was the most enjoyable; geography was interesting and marginally more successful for me; but economics remains a mystery to me even now! It was a miracle to pass all three in the end.

The first three years at Eton had been a tough grind and not a lot of fun. Things began to change in my A level years as I was about to turn sixteen. For one thing, I could give up the subjects I didn't like and focus on those where I had some interest. Secondly, after more than two years of non-contact sports, I could return to the playing fields and do what I loved. It was such a relief and I was able, slowly but surely, to relaunch myself and regain my confidence and identity. I threw myself into everything and soon established myself as a fearless tackler in rugby; the 'hard man' at Post in Eton's unique Field game and was head of the Ram – now banned on health and safety grounds, but essentially a line up of three boys who charged at the opposing team in their goal mouth to 'convert' a Rouge. You will be reaching for the Eton lexicon by now. However, most exciting was a whole new area of interest: the Combined Cadet Force.

The Eton CCF was one of the better resourced and supported units in the country with its own colours, presented by the Queen and a permanent adjutant from either the Guards or Green Jackets. It seemed to suit me perfectly, combining physical challenges with direct, hands-on leadership and personal skills training. I particularly enjoyed the exercises and deployments and loved patrolling, camping out in small tents (bashas) and generally reverting to the skulduggery I had perfected at MHS. I also found that I was quite good at it and soon got promoted to corporal and, in due course, sergeant and then cadet officer.

One early incident amused me when on exercise close to the main Salisbury Plain training area. I was put on sentry by a gate on a small country lane to provide lookout in case of any enemy infiltration. It was cold and rather boring, but, after about an hour, some car headlights came into view, which proved to be a small car travelling rather slowly. I was immediately on my guard. The car drew level with me and stopped a yard or two further on. I was now really on my mettle. A man got out and came directly towards me, lying by the gate, and I tried to make myself invisible up against the hedge, not moving a muscle. I was not expecting what happened next as the man unzipped his fly and was clearly about to take a leak right on top of me. "Excuse me!" I said, loudly, in a suitably plummy Eton accent. The man acted as if he had been electrocuted, jumping at least a foot in the air. He rushed back to his car and drove off with wheels spinning. Well, what would you do?

I began to enjoy CCF life more and more with assault courses, night manoeuvres and summer camps in Devon, and started seriously to consider the idea of a career in the army. The school adjutant at the time was a Grenadier Guards officer and he seemed the epitome of what I wanted to become. But it was at a Christmas drinks party in Cambridge, while staying with my cousins, that someone told me about the Commandos and the whole world of the Royal Marines. Suddenly, all I wanted was a green beret and gradually the path of my career began to take shape.

It was about this stage in school life that we had to attend interminable careers lectures about our futures. Life in the City or law or accountancy filled me with dread. I didn't have an estate to manage or a nice job in a family firm and the idea of prolonging my academic misery and going to university horrified me. Suddenly, there was really only one route – the military. So, at sixteen, and somewhat against the recommendation of the adjutant who wanted me to join the army, I applied for a 'reserved place' entry into the Royal Marines and went off to the Admiralty Interview Board ('AIB') in Gosport, Hampshire. It was the beginning of a new adventure, but I didn't get off to a very promising start! On arrival at the naval base, I somehow managed to get lost and entered the AIB induction programme backwards. That is to say, I entered by the exit door and started at the wrong end of the process, and everyone was confused as to who I was and why I hadn't seen anyone before them. They probably should have failed me there and then! The AIB involved numerous interviews with a variety of officers, psychiatrists, doctors, etc.; a complex analysis of a plane crash scenario with lots of factors that needed resolving; and a practical gym-based challenge over a water tank. I had no idea how I had performed other than that I fell in the water tank, but, to my delight, I received a letter three weeks later – they had accepted me! Now all I needed to get was my three A levels.

As I entered my final year at Eton, I felt much more settled and confident in myself and my future. I had some good friends, I had re-established my sporting credentials and I used the CCF to create a clear identity for myself. I quickly adopted Royal Marines vernacular and became known as 'the Commando', to which I didn't object. Being a cadet officer, I was allowed to wear 'stick-ups', a wing collar and bow tie, with my school uniform and although I was never cool enough to have been elected into 'Pop', the school's body of self-electing prefects, I felt I had achieved something (it was also invaluable to have learned how to tie a bow tie at such an early age). The final year of school also brought some privileges and I became a house prefect, known as being in 'the Library'. I also acquired a 'fag' – one of the new boys – who would tidy my room and fetch and carry for me. This rather derogatory name applied to boys in their first year who basically acted as unpaid slaves to the senior boys – and amazingly no one questioned it! Sadly, the days of 'Boy Calls' had ended a couple of years earlier when the inter-house telephone system was introduced. Boy calls were a primitive hangover from the early days, more akin to Tom Brown's school days, where a member of Library would shout "Boy up" and the last boy to get to him would get the job of delivering or collecting whatever was needed. Such calls were the bane of a junior boy's existence, carving into study time and being totally random. I remember one trip as a young thirteen-year-old, having to go to Windsor to collect something, which took over an hour out of my day. Mind you, woe betide any boy who tried to hide from a boy call! You will be glad to hear that fagging ended in the early 1980s.

Life at the top of the school was certainly more rewarding and at that time, our housemaster's wife happened to be the headmistress of Heathfield, the girls' school in Ascot. Some of the girls from Heathfield would attend classes at Eton where their subjects were not adequately covered, in particular physics and chemistry. These girls would come to our house for lunch, sitting with the boys on the top table. Unbelievably, these were some of my first interactions with girls, although discussing the pros and cons of potassium permanganate frankly didn't do it for me! However, sneaking a glimpse of a breast was much more exciting and almost more than I could cope with at that age, leading to a full debrief with the boys afterwards. After all, I was still only sixteen while others in my year had turned eighteen, could drive and needed to shave! I was still trying to catch up.

There was one episode at Eton which probably defines my time there and certainly the memories exchanged at house reunions ever since. It was the fire in my wastepaper basket. Before heading off to public school, Dad had done his best to give me a 'birds and bees' talk. It was a complete failure on every level, but of all the things he may have told me, the only thing I remember was about him telling me to watch out for my lamp! I was never really sure what he meant by this, but suspect that when he was at Eton, someone must have broken his lamp and he never forgot it. So, having been protecting my lamp with my life, I totally missed protecting my wastepaper bin! The mystery of who set fire to it has never been revealed and is the topic of speculation even now. All I know is that, along with my rather nice 1970s wood-effect, plastic bin, nearly 300 lines of Latin hexameters went up in smoke one day and then, to make matters worse, the housemaster blamed me. This incident happened in my O level year and since I was often getting into trouble at that time, I had prepared a stash of lines during my spare time. At Eton, instead of being asked to write conventional lines such as 'I must learn not do this or that...', the normal punishment was a chunk of Horace's georgics, namely Latin hexameters. This stash also served as a useful bartering tool if I was short of cash and others would buy them. Although I don't think the culprit will ever be revealed, for the record: I blame one of the 'naughty three', but will avoid pointing any further! But certainly the whole incident became part of RHP folklore and remains a curious anecdote to my Eton career.

My final half at Eton was Michaelmas 1974. I was seventeen and, having passed my A levels in the summer and been assured of my commission into the Royal Marines, I asked my father to let me stay for the extra Oxbridge term, even though I wasn't sitting the Oxbridge entrance exams. I regarded this time as a period of finishing school and growing-up time, since I also didn't want to head straight into the Royal Marines at seventeen. It was a sensible decision and allowed me to finish school on a high and enjoy the fruits of seniority. One of the side benefits was being the CCF platoon instructor for Mark, who rashly decided to try his hand at soldiering. Watching him try to march was always interesting, but I have one wonderful memory of leading him on a patrol when we heard the enemy coming round the corner. "Get off the track now," I said and jumped quickly to hide, unfortunately landing waist-deep in a water-filled trench and getting totally soaked. His laughter was uncontainable and, of course, very un-tactical! However, I went on to win the Recruit Instructor's Cup and we all celebrated. I think that was the occasion when I discovered that Pimm's could creep up in the system, unannounced, and then strike you down spectacularly with no notice!

We began to engage with the outside world a bit and there were trips to visit industry. I went to BP's headquarters and the Stock Exchange in London, and also the Huntley and Palmers biscuit factory in Reading. It was there that one our group won the jackpot on the slot machine in the staff canteen to the horror and undisguised envy of the workers sitting there, whose money had built up in the pot! We beat a hasty retreat – with the money.

It was a wrench saying our goodbyes after five years. The Eton way was to send 'leaver' photos to all of your friends. I still have my collection and amuse myself occasionally looking at the smiling and innocent faces beaming out at the camera. As parents have a habit of saying, 'school days are the best days of your life' and, in many ways, this is true. But squeezing the memories of ten years' worth of schooling into as many pages glosses over both the good and the bad times. I was no academic and didn't enjoy the theoretical process of learning. However, give me a practical reason or context for learning and I would jump at it, and this marked an important discovery for me. I think we were also lucky as a generation being spared the constant exam fever and school rankings process, which seems to create so much stress and non-stop pressure nowadays. We enjoyed long, lazy afternoons on the river, drinking cider at Queen's Eyot and sneaking a quick cigarette in the bushes on the way home. I made tables, bowls and a chessboard in the school of mechanics. I competed at Bisley in the school's Shooting VIII, firing .303 WWII rifles in the pre-ear defender age, when one's ears would still be ringing twenty-four hours later. Even the simple pleasure of running along the tow path on a frosty winter afternoon or kicking a ball around on Chambers field reminds me of a special time. All in all, it was an innocent and largely pre-drug existence, which allowed us to grow up at our own speeds, free from external interference, and for that I look back with gratitude and happiness at my school days.

Now for the next phase in life: Lympstone.

*MHS sports colours holders. David Gower is
on my left – c1966*

*Gymnastics display at MHS
– 1969*

Hurdling practice

Distant view of MHS from the dell

My acting highlight – the dead body in Billy Budd

A motley crew of RHP 6th formers

*After the
'Procession of
Boats', 4th June
1974 – St George*

*On a geography
field trip to
Durham – 1974*

Eton College Shooting VIII – 1974

Leaver's photo –
summer 1974

Chapter Three

The Royal Marines

I met Clive Richards at the Royal Marines medical board in London in early 1975 when I had just turned eighteen. It was a day that caused me to doubt all my decisions and whether I would even survive commando training. Clive was six feet five, weighed at least eighteen stone, was three years older than me and for the last year had been playing professional rugby in France. He was a giant of a man, with a worldly demeanour and confidence that I found breathtaking. He was the true incarnation of Captain Hurricane from the *Valiant* comic book, making me feel very much like Maggot Malone, his cartoon sidekick. What I didn't know until many years later was that while I went home wondering if I would survive, Clive went home equally nervous that all his fellow officers would be old Etonians or public schoolboys, and that he would be out of place as a state-schooled Essex boy. That we ended up such great long-term friends says much about the course on which we were both about to embark.

Officer Training

The Commando Training Centre at Lympstone in Devon is the spiritual home of the Royal Marines and a place of destiny for thousands of young men in search of an elusive green beret. But before I even arrived, I knew I had to try and toughen myself up after my rather cloistered existence at home and school. I had gone skiing over Christmas and New Year 1974/75 and came back broke after a brilliant holiday. I then spent three months working in the local petrol station, owned by a friend of ours, to make some money. I was grandly titled 'forecourt supervisor' and had two minions under me. Actually, the pump boys were great fun and we all used to ride around on our motorbikes visiting various unsafe pubs in High Wycombe. One day, one of the regular customers drove into the garage with his big Jaguar and then disappeared inside the showroom. Since his car was in the way, I jumped into the driving seat to move it, but managed to put it into reverse by mistake and I smashed into the car behind, which, unknown to me, had recently had a head-on crash, so was really smashed in. I couldn't believe my small bump could have caused so much damage and I was royally wound up by everyone. It was a fun time with a few surprisingly frisky women customers, making life fun and unpredictable.

My grand plan to toughen myself up was to walk from Land's End to John O'Groats. I went up to Lillywhites in London and bought myself some boots, a tent, a rucksack and all the kit, and a couple of days later travelled down to Cornwall. It was a glorious sunny day and I was feeling happy as I set off on my wonderfully romantic and virtually unplanned escapade. The first night I had a beautiful sleep and a great breakfast, and since I was sticking to footpaths and byways, I hardly encountered any traffic. The scenery was stunning and I had covered about forty miles by the third day, enjoying the novelty of being on my own and thinking about life and the universe – as one does on such occasions. But I had a problem with my new boots, which were giving me horrible blisters. The fourth day was grim and really impossible, and I simply didn't know how to deal with the blisters – now the size of a ten pence piece on each foot. Eventually I decided to cut the skin off, leaving two raw patches, which hurt even more. I had got to Truro, though! Not exactly the toughening-up adventure I had envisaged and now I could hardly walk. I decided to hitch a lift with two blokes heading for Bristol. After half an hour or so, they offered me a cigarette, which I thought would cheer me up. It was a new packet with a cellophane wrapping. I undid the pack and eventually lit my cigarette, but I hadn't put out the match properly, which then set fire to the cellophane in the ashtray and, before I knew it, I had managed to start a small bonfire on the back seat! They kicked me out a couple of hundred yards further on and frankly I felt lucky they hadn't beaten me up!

So now what? I made my way home and, for the first time in ages, was happy to have the refuge of home cooking and sympathy for a week or so. I shiver to think what my training sergeant would have said to me if he had ever found out about this phase in my life. It was quite bad enough that I was an old Etonian! The next few months were spent with my cousin, John Guillebaud, helping him redecorate and insulate his house in Oxford. It proved to be a perfect tonic and he taught me my now-famous party piece, 'Randycella' – the spoonerised version of Cinderella. But my feet remained a problem, having become infected and the site of the blister on my right foot having turned into a massive verruca. It was the start of a problem that afflicted me for the next year and all through commando training.

The summer of 1975 passed in a blur: the Henley Regatta, picnics, camping, parties and girls. It was a heady time, but the start date at Lympstone, 15th September, crept ever closer.

My rail warrant arrived and, with my suitcase packed with everything on the list, I headed off into the unknown. By great fortune, the first person I met at Exeter St David's station, where we changed onto the local Exmouth line, was Clive. We immediately concluded that we should stick together and help each other through the first few days. Lots of other nervous-looking, short-haired young men in suits also boarded the train and Clive and I quickly concluded that we probably weren't so out of place after all.

One of the real advantages of a public school education is that you get used to doing stupid things at odd times of the day and just take everything in your stride. At 6am the following morning, we were all awoken by shouted orders in the corridor and being told to be on the parade ground "NOW!" There followed our first of many 'beastings' – being run ragged around the assault course, lower field, estuary mud and then finally a dunk in the static water tank to clean off. An hour later and I think we had already lost one person off the course, and I laughed out loud to see one chap who had got dressed in his suit rather than PT kit and wondered if the suit would ever recover. But I didn't mind all this bullshit; in fact, I half expected it and found running and climbing a doddle, being a gymnast.

Unlike the army, where officers trained at Sandhurst, separate from the other ranks, all Royal Marines were trained at Lympstone and so we were unique in being immediately commissioned as probationary second lieutenants. This identified us from other recruits in blue and red berets and we had to be saluted along with any other officer, even though I suspect some of the trained ranks did so with a certain disdain. We also found that officers had to do exactly the same tests as the recruits but in faster times and this was part of the building of mutual respect that underpinned the whole approach to life in the Corps. Training followed a well-trodden and fairly predictable course. We were the elite UK force and so everything had to be perfect and standards were set very high. For the first ten weeks of basic training, we were all expected to become masters with iron and ironing board; for the first six weeks, we had to wash everything by hand, thereafter the washing machines became our best friends. We had to make bed packs every morning – this meant folding sheets and blankets in a specific way, which were then placed on our beds – and our rooms had to be immaculate. Being a naturally neat person, I was relieved to find that most of this was straightforward, albeit rather tiresome. But I was blessed to be in a cabin between two of the messiest and most disorganised individuals on the course: Steve on one side and John on the other. So, by comparison to whichever room the inspecting officer had just seen, my room was a veritable oasis of calm and tidiness, and this was incredibly lucky as I regularly saw the contents of either John's or Steve's rooms (or both) jettisoned through the window.

Our course officer was Captain Duncan Christie-Miller. He took on legendary status very quickly for his ability to give a bollocking and for his wonderfully dry sense of humour. His description (and verbal dismemberment) of one young officer's purple suit, complete with big '70s lapels and bell-bottom trousers, is memorable to this day. Duncan was 'old-school' in every sense, totally non-PC and a stickler for detail. He was also as tough as they come and knew how to motivate our disparate characters into a collective body, who stood or failed together. It took a bit of time to sink in, but we eventually realised that if we helped each other, we could hold out both against the training team and whatever hardship was being dished out at the time. This proved to be a very valuable lesson for life. Sadly, Duncan handed over his stewardship of our course after the initial phase of training and he was replaced by Captain Bertie Tailyour. Bertie was a career officer with something of a 'Marmite' personality, which some liked and others didn't. Bertie went on to command the Brigade so was clearly a very able officer and I liked him, although he was a completely different character to Duncan.

Initial training seemed to go on forever. It alternated between the parade ground, weapons handling, classroom lessons and field work. Drill was normally great fun as there were several uncoordinated individuals who simply couldn't march, however hard they tried, and they kept everyone else amused. Clive was doomed on the parade ground as his normal stride would have been about forty inches, so having to shorten this to the regular thirty-inch pace made him look as if he was always mincing rather than marching. Couple that with his ability to daydream and forget to listen for commands and it was a sure-fire disaster. One sunny Saturday morning, we were marching to the sound of the band; you could see Clive sticking his chest out with pride at everything he was doing and mincing down the parade ground, but failing to hear the command to halt. The drill instructor let him march off on his own for about 100 metres before shouting, "Come back, Mr Richards!" much to his embarrassment and our amusement.

Militarily, I found a lot of the basic training straightforward as it reinforced much of the CCF training at school. Patrolling came naturally and I enjoyed sneaking around and attacking unsuspecting recruits on Woodbury Common – the local training area. What I found harder was learning all the correct 'lingo' and right sequence for things, which otherwise seemed to be obvious to me. Military life certainly liked to complicate things, but the end of basic training was in sight and Christmas beckoned. What a relief from all the hassle, shouting, chasing around and pettiness. However, the next phase would make the last ten weeks seem like a holiday: commando training.

It is easy to understand why Prince Edward gave up at

this point when he was going through Royal Marines training a few years later. Eating mince pies and opening stockings at Sandringham would have been light years away from a week's tactical exercise on Dartmoor in the snow, and that is the reality of what awaited us shortly after we returned from the bosoms of our families in January 1976. Compared to the pre-Christmas training regime, which was largely about knocking a bunch of civvies into shape and establishing a basis of discipline and cohesion, tactical training was a significant step-change. Life became much harder and more demanding, and I think most of us went through moments of self-doubt and anxiety about whether we were really cut out for it. But this stage was the essential grounding of life as a Royal Marine as it tested us all equally, unwrapped from our backgrounds, privileges and the defensive 'walls' we all put up around ourselves. Training exposed our true personalities. Exhausted, deprived of sleep and challenged way beyond our natural comfort zones, we began to see each other as we truly were. There was nowhere to hide and the strength of individual characters began to stand out. Physical maturity and endurance were only part of the story and some were clearly stronger than others. What was far more revealing was the inner substance of determination, moral fibre and courage, which really defines a person and underpins the qualities needed by an officer to lead in combat. This process of individual catharsis created a foundation on which we could shape our own styles as officers. As the weeks progressed, we began to recognise a change in outlook, a maturity and a new-found confidence in each other. Those that couldn't step up quickly moved on and the course began to consolidate.

"It's mind over matter, Mr Madeley," I remember Sergeant Wilkins shouting. "I don't mind and you don't matter. Now crawl over here, you horrible little thing... Sir." I had made a rather silly mistake during bayonet practice on the ranges one freezing cold

February day. He had told us all to strip to the waist so that we could get some aggression in our bayonet fighting. I suggested that since it was a bit cold, perhaps we might keep our shirts on, whereupon he ordered me to strip to my underpants. It was ignominy on several levels. First, it was totally ludicrous and, indeed, laughable trying to look or act aggressively, charging dummies and thrusting my bayonet into sandbags, dressed in nothing but underpants and boots! Second, my underpants were light blue rather than the regulation green. It was a sin for which I had to go swimming in the estuary, crawl around in the mud and became known as 'powder blue' for much of the remainder of training, with all sorts of aspersions cast about Etonians as you can imagine. Mind you, it was preferable to poor Jerry Thomas, a fellow young officer, who was singled out by Sergeant Wilkins for a rather realistic bayonet fight and was stabbed through the foot!

All of this was simply a prelude to the commando course, which began in March and lasted for six weeks. With the pace of military and tactics training increasing daily, the commando course added an additional physical element, which brought most of us to our knees by the end. There was a minimum of three hours' physical training every day with speed marches getting longer and more demanding. There are four commando tests that every marine and officer must pass to earn the right to wear a green beret. These are: a nine-mile speed march to be completed in ninety minutes; the endurance course – a six-mile course over bog, rough terrain, a water tunnel and roads – to be completed in seventy minutes; the 'Tarzan assault course' – a ropes and agility course followed by the assault course and thirty-foot wall – to be completed in eleven minutes; and finally, the thirty-miler across Dartmoor to be completed under seven hours. All the tests are carried out with full fighting order and rifle, which weigh about thirty-five pounds. I should point out that on our course, the thirty-miler was not run as such but incorporated into the final commando course exercise on Dartmoor and it is debateable whether the exercise or the actual run was tougher. Either way, these tests were the pinnacle of our training and the determination to win a green beret became palpable.

The blue beret with its red flash under the cap badge was discarded in favour of a WWII style cap comforter, which looked like an upside-down sock on our heads! It marked all trainees on their commando course and created a special identity. For me, the hardest part of the overall training was the 200m fireman's carry. My partner was a good two stone heavier than me and I struggled to complete this in the ninety seconds allotted. For others, the full regain on the rope over the static tank was a killer. This involved shinning along the rope and then swinging your legs fully off to hang below and then getting back on top of the rope and continuing across. Clive, in particular, struggled with this since by the time he had swung his legs off, they were well underwater in the tank. But ultimately all the tests required running and, thank goodness, I was a strong runner and every person who dropped out only strengthened my resolve to keep going. I could never understand how people could drop out with less than a mile to go. What made everything harder for me was dealing with the large verruca on my right foot, which was rather like running with a drawing pin in your boot. Each morning I would carefully place a ring of cushioning around the verruca, which would take the worst of the pressure. However, it wasn't pleasant and I knew that once the commando course was finished, I would have to get it dealt with.

The pride we all felt as we marched up to receive our green berets is impossible to express. It was the culmination of six months of the hardest basic training of any regular force in the world and the standards have resolutely been maintained since the first green berets were awarded in Achnacarry during the war. I was just nineteen years old. Mum and Dad watched as we returned from the nine-miler, grey with fatigue, but triumphant in our demeanour. It was the end of a key phase in our training and, undoubtedly, a watershed in our maturity both as individuals and collectively as officers. It was the making of me in so many ways, although far from the toughest challenge that I have faced since.

After the intensity of the first six months, the second half of training felt more like a holiday, although woe betide anyone who was late or hadn't prepared properly. But the physical pressure was off and we were treated with the respect that accompanies a green beret. Tactics developed from section and troop manoeuvres to company, commando (battalion level) and brigade operations. Specialist skills in signals, advanced weapon handling, explosives, cliff assault techniques, etc. filled our day and we began to see how our core skills could be deployed to advantage by infiltration and subversion. We spent time on landing craft and with the Special Boat Service (SBS) in Poole – the latter made a very strong impression on me as being the pinnacle of the commando role and it was something to which I returned a few years later. Our field exercises became more testing from a leadership perspective and we regularly worked with other recruits under training, knowing that many might serve under us in our first commando unit. There were plenty of valuable learning experiences, which, more often than not, were the result of our own cock-ups.

And suddenly, training was all over! After a long final exercise in Germany involving a brutal 'advance to contact' over twenty kilometres and an 'escape and evasion' phase, most of which I sadly missed having had the second (and successful) operation to excavate my verruca, we formed up on the parade ground for the last time. It was a special day, second only to being awarded our green berets, and I remember feeling like a very big brother to Sue and Mark who attended the pass out. I was posted to 42 Commando at Bickleigh Barracks on the edge of Dartmoor, along with eight others from the course, and this was to be our next adventure.

Commando Service

I can still remember the smell of the aviation fuel and the warm wind whipped up by the blades of the Wessex V helicopter as John Mason, John Sugden and I, the three new troop commanders in K Company, 42 Commando, waited to board and fly out to join our respective troops. We were weighed down with our kit and rifles and, for the first time, realised that training was over and how we conducted ourselves in the next few weeks could define our time as young officers.

We were joining our troops on board HMS *Hermes* in the North Sea and being launched straight into a two-week NATO exercise in Denmark and Norway. Flying in from Scotland to a carrier underway at sea and taking over one's first command a few moments later was a special experience and probably the best way to get stuck in. We were immediately put to work and had to draw on everything we had learned at Lympstone as we went through a variety of different evolutions during the Denmark phase. I led my first troop attack and several fighting patrols and felt immediately at home in my new role. Importantly, it allowed the thirty men of my troop to check me out as a leader and I wasn't going to let them down. Possibly more challenging than the exercises in Denmark and Norway was the twenty-four-hour 'run ashore' in Amsterdam. Seven hundred marines in uniform all heading for the red-light district is a sight to behold. I had never seen anything like it!

It would become tedious to chronicle every step as a first-year young officer. There were some highs and lows and some memorable moments at 42 Commando, and we all became a tight team. The 'subaltern's friend' was John Mason, who, due to various and repeated misdemeanours, managed to clock the most extra duties as duty officer. On one famous occasion, 150 rounds of live ammunition and two hand grenades were found in his cabin during an inspection by the adjutant. It was a record even for him, but meant that everyone else had rather more shore leave than he did. In a strange way, we were all exploring our new freedom as grown-ups since none of us had been to university, having joined straight from school with very little worldly experience.

One moment is worth recording, however, when K Company was tasked to be the assault force on one of the North Sea oil rigs. These rigs were deemed to be a likely terrorist target and so we needed to train regularly to develop the requisite skills to recapture them, which was a considerable challenge. We travelled to Scotland and went through endless rehearsals with the specialists until we were certain we could do it in our sleep. On the day of the attack, however, there was a huge snowstorm and the helicopters were grounded. We needed to entertain the troops and decided that a snowman-building competition was the answer. All sorts of shapes and sizes emerged, including some rather phallic offerings, and the latter became a target for the RAF police in their Ford Sherpa patrol van. The police van would drive directly at the snowmen, knocking them for six, and then disappear with much satisfaction. It didn't take long for a wise old marine to build the next big snowman around one of the various water hydrants scattered about the barracks. On cue, the RAF van turned up and, with much relish, charged at the snowman. The resultant crash, water plume and demolished van was more than we could have hoped for and we went back to our barracks in high spirits, leaving two very red-faced young

RAF policemen to face the music. By the way, we attacked the oil rig the next day very successfully!

Life in barracks can often be a challenge to motivate and occupy energetic marines and I wanted to do something on my own for my own troop, rather than being part of the normal company training. I arranged two specific exercises, the first being to the Brecon Beacons, where we did our version of the 'Fan Dance' – the infamous SAS selection test – up and down Pen y Fan. It was February and very cold, but fantastic to be completely immersed with the troop and working together. It was a great success and spurred me to organise a second adventure for the troop. This time, I decided to organise an amphibious raid on Guernsey in the Channel Islands, involving landing craft, small boats and an infiltration across the island before blowing up an old WWII bunker. The enemy was supposed to be the local CCF, but, in fact, almost the entire island turned out to look for us. It was an adventure in lots of ways, including one moment when I jumped over a low wall, only to fall twenty feet on the other side to avoid being seen by an oncoming car. However, as another chance to strengthen the sense of team spirit and also collect a huge haul of duty-free (no, that wasn't the real reason), it was a great success.

Towards the end of my year in 42 Commando, we headed off to the West Indies. One of the war-time roles of the Royal Marines was to secure the Atlantic Islands resupply chain and I wasn't about to argue about a trip to the sun. We headed off to Vieques, a US Marine Corps training island off the coast of Puerto Rico. It wasn't quite Jamaica, but it was still great fun and we managed to experiment with almost every phase of war over the three weeks we were there. The entire eastern end of the island was a live firing range and we could, and did, fire every type of weapon held by the unit, which was very impressive. Almost as impressive was the size of the hole we had to dig to bury one unfortunate cow who ventured onto range and provided the opportunity for a bullet penetration demonstration.

The local nightlife was also quite colourful, with piña coladas proving to be my new favourite drink. However, the locals themselves were a fiery lot and the supposedly peaceful Vieques was where I was shot at for the first time. My troop had managed to upset the locals by chatting up one of the local girls and her irate boyfriend began shooting at us with an M16 Armalite rifle. Bullets were flying everywhere and, in a slightly drunken state, I thought I should go and sort it out. I took a few steps down the road with car windscreens shattering all around me, before one of my marines pulled me to the ground out of the way. We were escorted back to camp by twenty armed US Marines and were, unfortunately, banned from town for the rest of the trip. How none of us was hit was a miracle.

1977 was the Queen's Silver Jubilee year and, as part of the celebrations, 42 Commando provided a Guard of Honour on Plymouth Hoe. It was a ceremonial highlight and I was asked to be the escort to the young princes, Andrew and Edward (sixteen and fourteen, respectively). It was a privilege and, although only a few years older than them, I felt very proud to show them around the stands and explain everything. It was ironic that ten years later I would be in Prince Edward's training team when, ill-advisedly, he attempted Royal Marines (RM) training. My only disappointment that day was not to have been awarded one of the Silver Jubilee medals. Due to general defence economies at the time, the entire unit were only given six medals and I was way down the list!

I had had a successful first command and was, undoubtedly, a bit cocksure as I headed off to my next assignment. I received a very good report and felt ready for anything. But the fact was that I was still only twenty years old and not very experienced. Sure, I was fit enough and was as dogged as the next person in any endurance challenge, but I wasn't hardened by experience. All I wanted to do was to go for SBS selection and challenge myself with what I saw as the ultimate military role. What I really needed was time to grow up a bit and, after a spell at the Britannia Royal Naval College, Dartmouth, completing what we called our 'joined-up writing course', I headed to 41 Commando and Belfast for my first Northern Ireland tour.

You will be reassured to know that before troops were let loose in Northern Ireland, they had to spend several weeks training for this very different type of military activity. Military Aid to the Civil Community (MACC) was an evolving concept in the 1970s, with some spectacular and rather tragic learning experiences in Bloody Sunday, Operation Motorman and others. I took over the mortar troop of support company, where many of my marines and non-commissioned officers (NCOs) were on their seventh or eighth tour. There was no shortage of experts or advice and, suddenly, my inexperience was very plain. The training at the Lydd and Hythe training grounds in Kent certainly exposed my naivety and – compared to conventional operations – terrorist activity, deceit, subterfuge and having to operate within a strict set of rules of engagement presented a much more complex set of leadership and soldiering challenges. It also made me much more aware of the very protected life I had enjoyed at home and school with no exposure to the hatred, ignorance, poverty and ugliness that was daily life for so many in Northern Ireland (and elsewhere) in the 1970s. This was raw and personal, and the dangers were far more tangible and real than anything I had previously encountered. Being shot was the least of it; the bigger worries were being separated from the rest of the team and attacked or being maimed by an IED (improvised explosive device). Suddenly, soldiering became real for me.

In early 1978, West Belfast was still a hotbed of sectarian

violence with Bobby Sands dying that year and Gerry Adams and Martin McGuinness both 'arrest on sight' targets. We took over from the Coldstream Guards, who had lost three men in their four-month tour and one officer who had been brutally glassed and knifed while making an arrest in a pub on the Falls Road. My company commander was a control freak who micromanaged the next four months for us. It was the opposite of the freedoms I had enjoyed in 42 Commando and suddenly I had to justify everything I did at exactly the moment when I suddenly no longer felt so confident about what I was doing. It was a tough learning experience, working out how to keep a difficult boss happy while also managing my troop and my own sanity – strangely valuable lessons that I was to draw on twenty years later in the banking world.

Our company 'patch' was an area bordered by the Ballymurphy estate in the west, the Donegal Road and Celtic football ground, leading up to the Divis Flats in the north and by Andersonstown and the Turf Lodge estate in the south. It was in the heart of bandit country, with the Falls Road running south to north through the middle of it. The area was depressing and run-down with graffiti everywhere and the stench of poverty. Houses were long rows of 'two-up, two-down' terraced blocks with a back alley behind them, strewn with dustbins, broken-down cars and rubbish. It was grim patrolling the area and must have been even worse to live there with little hope of breaking free.

The locals had grown ambivalent to the presence of troops and mostly tried to stay out of trouble. There were a few unrelenting nationalists who were as entertaining as they were threatening; the 'Bionic Granny' being one. She would hurl abuse at every patrol who came anywhere near her house in an area known as the Rodneys, banging the ground with dustbin lids, shouting and throwing buckets of water at us. It was generally harmless banter, but we were always alert to the classic 'come on' – a distraction designed to draw troops into an area where a sniper would then have a shot at someone. But our patrolling was designed to thwart such tactics by having multiple small foot patrols swamp an area so that the locals would never know who was where. We also had a section on QRF (quick reaction force) at the base who would leap into their Land Rovers to provide instant support. The idea of these ancient Land Rovers getting anywhere faster than about thirty-five mph didn't seem odd at the time and, of course, they were very exposed in such circumstances, especially as they entered and exited the base, as was proven when one marine was shot in the back a few months later. Luckily, he survived as the 5.56mm Armalite round bounced off a rib and deflected away from his heart and out via his shoulder!

Strangely enough, we all wanted to be involved in an incident as it provided a distraction from the boredom of street patrolling and the endless cordon and search tasks. One evening, a Harp Lager lorry was hijacked on the Springfield Road, Falls Road junction, and there was a good old riot going on. It was one of the few occasions to get stuck in and some scores were settled during the evening. Fortunately, only stones and bottles were being thrown, rather than anything more lethal, and my troop used the time to liberate a couple of crates of beer off the lorry for a party afterwards, little knowing that we could have been done for looting!

There was only one time that I was really frightened and, looking back over my life, it was probably the single most threatening moment I have ever experienced. I was tasked to arrest a suspect who was known to be having a drink in an illegal pub close to our base. I went into the hall with my Int Corporal and we walked around inside to look for our man. There were about fifty to sixty locals inside and so I positioned a big marine with a baton gun just inside the door to deter any brave locals from trying anything on. But as the corporal and I walked around and were at the furthest point from the door, the locals began to bang their glasses on the tables and the situation was rapidly turning ugly. The next thing would have been someone hitting the fuse box and plunging us all into darkness, whereupon we would have been attacked with knives, broken glass and anything else to hand. I had left my rifle outside as I didn't want to be hampered with something unwieldy in close quarters, so only had my fists for protection. I called on my radio and three more marines quickly came inside and, suddenly, the mood changed, but I realised that it had been a close call and not a situation I wanted to find myself in again. But we got our man and arrested him outside, then despatched him of to Castlereagh – the now notorious police interrogation centre.

There were a few lighter moments inevitably, such as using our high-powered telescopes to watch the young nurses in the Royal Victoria Hospital accommodation block or using night-vision scopes to catch young couples testing the suspension on cars around the back alleys. It lightened the mood a bit, but as we neared the end of our tour, I was struck with an underlying sense of futility about the conflict and the role of the army in trying to police the province when so many intractable religious and political issues remained. All of us were happy to hand over to the incoming army regiment and board the ship out of Belfast docks to return to Deal, without a single life lost, for some well-deserved R&R. It had been quite a learning experience for me on both a personal and professional level, and I was glad to have picked up the medal and the status that went with it.

Special Boat Service

Returning from leave in May 1978, I confirmed that I wanted to attend selection and training for the Special Boat Service, which had so captured my imagination during young officer training. It was, for me, the ultimate challenge and, even though still only twenty-one, I felt ready. Having spent the preceding weeks running around Deal with increasingly heavy bergans trying to build up my fitness and stamina, I drove to RM Poole in June for the four-week pre-selection course. This initial programme was designed to weed out those who were not good swimmers, didn't like diving and/or couldn't cope with being cold, wet and completely knackered. It is hard to imagine how four weeks could seem so long. During the period, we clocked up over a thousand minutes underwater and were run ragged when on the surface. Mud, sea and sand became our habitat, and personal determination was the only thing that enabled any of us to keep going. But we all knew it was just a taster for the course proper, which would start after summer leave. A reduced group of about twelve of us had made it through. This was 'grown-up soldiering'. There were no sergeants shouting at us or endless inspections, although woe betide anyone falling short on basic disciplines, cleanliness or professionalism. It was all about effective small-team tactics, specialist roles and unconventional warfare. The essence of Special Forces soldiering is independence of outlook, physical and mental robustness, self-confidence and self-sufficiency, all underpinned by a strong sense of team identity and commitment.

The twelve-week Swimmer Canoeist III (SC3) course began by testing all of us on an individual level. The intensity of swimming, unarmed combat, map reading, load carrying and endurance steadily escalated over the early weeks. Each day started with a 6am PT session, which, in a normal world, would be enough physical activity for a week, let alone the start of a single day! We had Australian SAS and US SEAL officers and NCOs on the training team, and there appeared to be a competition between them as to who could make our training the hardest. But Captain Richard Clifford, the diminutive officer who had parachuted into the Atlantic to defuse a bomb on the Queen Elizabeth II liner, was our course officer and a tougher individual you would be hard put to find. He seemed to dismiss anyone who hadn't sailed the Atlantic single-handed, canoed round the UK or endured something equally impossible, and I think he made an immediate judgement about me. I was hopelessly immature in comparison to this man, even in a world of rapid change in Special Forces tactics and the need for new skills.

Canoe training was, undoubtedly, the hardest phase of SBS training. The Klepper was a canvas and wooden canoe that could be collapsed and carried in two loads, one being the rubber and canvas 'skin' and the other being the wooden 'stringers'. Each load weighed about 100 pounds, although the skin gained at least another fifteen pounds when wet. We made progressively longer trips, interspersed with long portages where we carried the collapsed canoes and all our kit and rifles. Trying to be tactical when carrying over 120 pounds on your back is like expecting a turtle to do an agility course. It was brutal!

One day, we canoed from Poole harbour around the coast to Lulworth Cove, negotiating the violent rip tide off St Alban's Head, where waves were about fifteen to twenty feet high. One canoe, with two of the toughest members on the course, capsized and we had to raft up to help them bail out and climb back in. The remaining journey to Lulworth was tough enough, but when we arrived, we were told that there would be a race to Wool Train Station (about six miles up the hill). The two who had capsized gave up at that point, which was really unexpected, but made me realise that this course was as much about mental toughness as it was physical. My canoe partner and I won the 'race' up the hill, only to be faced with the next task, and so it went on.

Specialist training provided welcome distraction from the daily slog of canoeing and endurance training. Demolitions, signals (including Morse code), first aid, caching skills (burying and retrieving equipment), close reconnaissance missions, work with agents and escape lines, etc. provided a glimpse of the world beyond training. The course gradually reduced in size, although the pace of training seemed to pick up. One fearsome day involved canoeing from Portsmouth to Ryde on the Isle of Wight, a portage across to Sandown and then another 'race' to the Nab Tower (about ten miles offshore), before a tow from a submarine back into Portsmouth. The day concluded with a limpet attack on a warship anchored in the harbour with all the crew on lookout. The oxygen re-breather sets we used don't leave any bubbles, so stealth was the key objective and we succeeded in placing four limpets between us – a job well done.

The final exercise was a classic SBS mission. Four canoes were dropped off in the Channel from an oiler in a force 6 sea, which, in itself, was a major challenge. Getting into the canoes as they rose and fell fifteen feet next to the side of the ship required immaculate timing and a lot of nerve, not least to avoid dropping one's rifle or anything else important! We then canoed about fifteen miles to the Isle of Sheppey to conduct a close recce of the prison on the island. We had to sneak past the local police and take a series of night photographs with specialist cameras before canoeing and portaging around to the Medway to an observation point where we would plan an attack on the Isle of Grain oil refinery. The attack two days later involved four assault teams breaching the perimeter fencing and security patrols and each placing demolition charges. We then withdrew to a rendezvous point before dispersing to be passed down an escape line back to Poole. It was the culmination of everything we had trained for and was as tough as anything we had done to date. It was pure commando work and exactly what I had joined for.

After nearly five months, the course had become a tight-knit team. We had learned our inner strengths and weaknesses beyond anything we could have imagined during basic training. We had confronted depths of exhaustion and personal vulnerabilities and learned how to support each other during the low points. It was, in fact, an incredible journey of self-discovery. It made the news that I wasn't selected to continue with further specialist training and full-time work with the SBS even harder to accept. Yet as I look back, it was really the only logical conclusion to have reached at the time. I was as fit and determined as the best of them, but I didn't have the experience or maturity to draw on and, as the Commanding Officer (CO) said to me, I was sent on the course too soon. The same man was my CO four years later and I very nearly decided to go through it all again to fulfil my determination to be an SBS officer. The process of saying goodbyes to those who remained was tough, but a wonderful mutual respect and trust had grown between us and we knew that we had all achieved something very special, even if not all of us would continue to serve in the SBS. I bumped into Mick M, my canoe buddy, twenty years later in London and he said he was very sad that I hadn't been taken on. He ended up as the SBS Regimental Sergeant Major (RSM) and thought I could have made a great troop leader. Ah well!

Army exchange

So, with my immediate military career goal frustrated, I wondered what was next. I was sent back to Lympstone to take a recruit troop through training, which was a useful distraction and a reminder of the core values on which the Corps is based and is so rightly proud. I found that my SBS training gave me an even stronger sense of personal commitment to professional standards and leadership, and I determined that I would live the SBS values as best I could. My troop was passed for duty by HRH Prince Philip, our Captain General, and his dry (some would say, caustic) sense of humour was immediately apparent as he inspected the ranks and cracked jokes about all and sundry. He was very irreligious and not at all what I had expected, but I was proud that my recruits were passed out by him with parents and friends watching.

The news that my next appointment was to be a secondment to the army was unexpected. I was to be sent to the British Army on the Rhine (BAOR) to join 1 Queens, a mechanised infantry unit with whom the Royal Marines had shared a historical link as they had previously served as marines on board ships. I remember driving out to Germany in my yellow Triumph Spitfire with all my kit, wondering what awaited me and realising that for the next two years I would represent the Royal Marines in everything I did. It was a lot to live up to. I was twenty-two years old with only four years' service under my belt and heading into a completely new world. The fact that, nearly forty years later, the gang of subalterns I joined still meet up regularly is testament to the friendships, experiences and antics we shared.

As events transpired, I had, by great fortune, joined a battalion that was on top of its game, having been operating as a mechanised battle group for over four years and led from the front by an outstanding, charismatic, no-nonsense CO. The unit had an *esprit de corps* and sense of purpose about it that instantly made me feel at home. Mech warfare was an eye-opener and the battalion were very proficient, giving me many valuable lessons for a later role when, as adjutant, I ran

42 Commando's CP (command post) from tracked over-snow vehicles in Norway. You could cover great distances quickly and use the ground and speed to tactical advantage. However, as I soon discovered, sitting in the back of an APC could be very disorientating and so a greater weight of responsibility rested on the officers and NCOs whose heads were sticking up in the turrets and could actually see what was going on. The result was a motivated and switched-on cadre of leaders, but sometimes some less enthusiastic, disoriented and seasick soldiers in the back.

My platoon sergeant was a colourful cockney with a wry sense of humour and he and I got along famously, at least that's what he told me! We had many amusing moments together, including one occasion when we were waiting in our APCs on the start line for a night attack. I was dozing on the engine louvres (a nice place to keep warm) when the signal finally came through. I was half asleep and leapt up, only to fall off the side of the vehicle. Unfortunately, the radio headset and microphone unit were hanging around my neck, which then acted like a hangman's noose as I went over the side. I bit my tongue half through, so when I opened the back of the APC door to give the orders, I was frothing blood and must have looked truly wild.

I was keen to try and make my platoon a bit different and we painted fouled anchors on the vehicles and started to use a few RM expressions to confuse others. I was also keen to give the soldiers a break from being driven everywhere and we took every opportunity to go on foot patrols, which was always a challenge in the featureless desert that is the Soltau training area. Good map reading was essential, given that tracked vehicles very quickly made a nonsense of most features shown on a map. Our close recce troop commander from the 15th/19th Hussars got the award for map-reading incompetence; following him was entertaining at times and more out of curiosity than with any real confidence that he knew where he was going. The CO seemed to have grown used to sixty tanks and armoured vehicles trying to make a U-turn in narrow forest rides in the middle of the night! One of my last sightings of him was in the middle of a large swamp, slowly sinking in his Scimitar, as the rest of the battle group bypassed the bog and continued on its way.

The BAOR exercises were on a different scale to those I had experienced before, with the military effectively able to drive wherever they liked, using actual towns and villages in a tactical way as if in a real war. Needless to say, the damages paid out to the locals could be significant, but it led to a far more realistic approach to training and we would regularly train over the actual ground that would be our responsibility if the Soviets poured over the Inner German Border ('IGB'). I later went on a special IGB patrol where we would monitor the 'Wall' from the west and see all the automatic machine guns, minefields and watch towers. It is hard to imagine now just how hostile and alien it was. The East German guards seemed particularly interested in me and my green beret, probably wondering how I had managed to get so lost!

Albuhera Barracks, our home in Werl, a small German village in Westphalia, looked a bit 'post-war functional' than anything seen these days, but was well placed for the trappings and distractions of Dortmund, Hamm and elsewhere. Down the road was the Möhnesee and dam that had so famously been bombed by the Dambusters during WWII. It was not unheard of to see a group of enthusiastic (and slightly inebriated) subalterns marching in goose steps over the dam, whistling the theme tune from the movie, much to the bemusement of the locals.

Socially, life was full, and the availability of very cheap alcohol in the NAAFI (the canteen) and the messes meant that the camp became much more of a home for its inhabitants than would normally be the case in a UK-based establishment. As subalterns, we were constantly pushing the boundaries of behaviour and adventure (*plus ça change*), but generally acted just within acceptable limits. Carrying the padre's Mini into the dining room was borderline and the oil stain it left on the carpet cost us all a chunk of pay the following month. But high spirits were the name of the game and we were all up for it, and I was determined not to let the Royal Marines down. Sometimes, my desire to show the way didn't end well. My demonstration of how to dismount from the roof of the mess by doing a forward roll off the gutter somehow played out better in my head than it did in practice! But in all this bravado and juvenile activity, we subalterns became great friends, and whether playing rugby against the nearby unit, on a 'run ashore' to the local pub or competing to see how fast we could consume a pizza, we supported each other unquestioningly.

Absence of female company added a certain frisson to life in Werl and created some interesting situations (more fully explored in a subsequent chapter). But the weekly trip to the Tropicana public swimming pool complex in Dortmund deserves mention. The Germans seem to love to go naked whenever they can and Thursday evening was nude night at the Tropicana! For a bunch of over-sexed twenty-year-olds, these sessions were hysterical and we would regularly follow pretty young girls into the Tropicana only to struggle to find them later among the acres of wobbly flesh on the other side of the changing rooms. On one occasion, we found a giant whirlpool bath where a large German man was standing astride a powerful jet, which was clearly giving him some pleasure. I decided to stand behind him and put my foot over the jet to deprive him of his titillation and see what happened. Unfortunately, the jet was so powerful that my foot was blasted right up his bottom and my big toe clearly found a particularly intimate place judging by the expression on his face, as was later reported to me. We beat a hasty retreat with much laughter.

Life in Germany proved to be a wonderful tonic for me on every level. Professionally, I learned a lot from my introduction to mech warfare and the speed and distances across which battle groups and brigades could respond, and I developed considerable respect for the quick thinking, clear leadership and soldiering competence across the unit. So much for the 'Pongo' stories I had been fed on back at home! I was also at ease with my fellow officers and the camaraderie we enjoyed then, and still enjoy forty years later, remains very important. The move back to Canterbury in mid 1980 was welcome but also marked the end of the special cohesion we had enjoyed in BAOR and a number of new appointments, including a new CO, marked a fresh start. The immediate goal was a six-month tour in Belize and specialist jungle training. Professionally, this was an interesting transition for the soldiers, who had to adapt from being delivered in an APC to the enemy objective and instead had to patrol on foot through dense jungle. The Belizean jungle was all secondary, that is to say it was thick with undergrowth and smaller trees, which had to regrow after each hurricane hit it. Belizean jungle was particularly thick and dirty, and one feature was a very unpleasant tree with two-inch spines all over the bark. We called it the 'Bastard Tree', because, invariably, if you lost your footing and grabbed out for support, you would find a bastard tree – hence the exclamation. The spines could be very dirty and would cause bad infections if not removed.

The first phase for all platoon commanders and NCOs was a training camp with the local SAS troop. Three weeks in the jungle was a great way to get into a routine and we all adapted quickly, oblivious to the growing and penetratingly awful smell we acquired over the period through sweat, dirt and a 'no washing' policy. Rations were predominantly tinned, but occasionally we would get something fresh. On one occasion, we cornered a baby wild pig and were closing in to finish it off when 'Mummy' appeared around the corner, sending us diving for cover as she clearly wasn't amused! We did get helicopter resupply drops from time to time and I remember one such drop when mail was also delivered. I was the only person not to receive any correspondence at all, not even a bank statement or 'Dear John' letter. I had clearly alienated all girlfriends at the time and even my parents! Incidentally, in good military form, a rather cringing 'Dear John' letter was shared around, which helped soften the blow for the unfortunate recipient.

Throughout Belize, there were Mayan ruins – many of which had been salvaged from the jungle. These magnificent temples would suddenly confront you on patrol, rather like something out of *Raiders of the Lost Ark*, and it made for a special experience. Snakes and spiders were less welcome and Belize had plenty. It was not uncommon to share a shower stall with a large tarantula and, as I can attest, they often jump when provoked, which can be a big surprise first time! Other creepy-crawlies made for amusing tricks at night in our bashas. One poor chap had a very vivid imagination and so we would pretend to be wild pigs in the undergrowth near his hammock. We probably risked being shot as we larked around, but it kept us amused even if it wasn't very tactical sometimes. Rather unfairly, we laid a jam trail up to his hammock on the last evening and watched the electrifying commotion as his hammock, bedding and clothes were overrun with ants in the middle of the night.

Barracks life in Belize was rather restrictive with little outside amusement. But there was a nearby river, complete with rapids and waterfalls, which made for a good R&R barbeque and overnight spot. Soldiers are reasonably easy to please, provided there is enough beer. Belize City was a bit of a dump in 1980, although I gather it is now quite an exotic holiday destination.

But there were local markets and shops and plenty of distractions for young soldiers. More interesting were the islands on the big offshore reef, which ran the full length of the country. These islands were idyllic with shanty bars and dive centres on most of them to explore the reef, which was truly spectacular. I also enjoyed plenty of water skiing in the offshore mangrove islands. These natural and calm waterways made for perfect waterskiing, provided you cleared them out first of any sharks or crocodiles who wanted to rest there. This was normally easy enough by driving the ski boat up and down the main stretches a couple of times. However, there were a few occasions when dolphins liked to play along with the ski boat, which could be very unsettling if you happened to be the guy on the end of the rope.

All too soon, and after a trip back to Europe for skiing, the Belize tour drew to an end. But just before we were about to leave, the locals decided to start rioting and disrupting the generally peaceful life in Belize. I don't remember the reasons, but a state of emergency was declared and we were all posted to different parts of the city. Riots soon started and everyone became quite excited, especially the local police force, who saw this as a chance for some payback. Tragically, though, while I was sitting in one of the police stations, a visiting inspector failed to unload his pistol correctly and discharged a round into a young constable sitting opposite. There then followed a tragic farce of incompetence as paramedics and colleagues tried in vain to insert a drip into his arm while he lost consciousness and then, a few minutes later, died. It cast a sad shadow on what had otherwise been a varied and interesting tour, and reminded me again of the proximity to violence that is the soldier's duty.

My time with 1 Queens ended shortly after our return to Canterbury in the spring of 1981. One highlight of the year being the marriage of my great friend, Clive, and Mary Anne in Kenton parish church. How he managed to hook such a lovely bride still eludes me! For me, it was a return to the bosom of the Royal Marines after two years on secondment. As much as I had enjoyed and benefitted from my time with the army, I was first and foremost a Royal Marine and I wanted to build my career there. I feared I might have been 'out of sight and therefore out of mind' when it came to interesting appointments within the Corps. In fact, this wasn't the case (as you will see), but the urge to re-embed within the Corps was strong.

Although covered in a subsequent chapter, I should also record for the sake of contemporaneous reference that, having met her earlier in the year while skiing in the Alps, I married Debbie on 19th December 1981, bringing to an end my rather wayward single life. It was supposed to be the start of a stable married career, even though events didn't quite work out that way.

Staff duties

I was just shy of twenty-five years old and had enjoyed a remarkably active career with over four years as a troop commander in a variety of theatres. Life finally caught up with me in January 1982 and I was appointed as aide de camp (AdC) to the major general in command of training, reserve and special forces, based at Eastney, Portsmouth. It seemed impossibly bad luck that after four years as a troop commander, with all that accumulated experience, I was starting a staff job just as the Falklands War started. The only person who seemed pleased that I wasn't travelling down to the South Atlantic was my mother. Ironically, the general I was working for was a bull of a man and an ex-SBS officer, and he tried every trick in the book to find a role for us. Furthermore, his command included NP 8901, the Falklands garrison, and we were due to have made a visit had the war not started. He and I quietly fumed that we were missing out on a classic amphibious operation and justification for all the training we had endured. While he had served in various conflicts, I wanted to prove myself in active service and it was a bitter disappointment to be left behind, along with the other half of the Corps and, of course, most of the army. However, I learned about the importance of the support activities and sadly also of the welfare work that crucially supports overseas operations, being closely involved with breaking the news of the death of a gallant young corporal to his new wife left behind in Portsmouth. Once again, the reality of death and uncertainty was very sobering.

However, being an AdC proved to be an interesting insight into higher command activities and perspectives, and I accompanied my general on a variety of interesting tours and presentations even though I was there mainly as his personal bag carrier rather than anything more important. But proximity to a senior officer and his conversations was very insightful and we ended up good friends. I was very upset to learn that he died four years after retiring from the Corps, aged only sixty. His successor was Julian Thompson, the brigadier who had masterminded the Falklands campaign, and he was to prove a superb and patient mentor to me both during my service and subsequently. Julian was a remarkable man who instilled a practical and down-to-earth approach to leadership, yet backed up with steely resolve and professionalism. He was the epitome of a Royal Marines officer and I have tried to emulate him in many ways since. He taught me that popularity was not necessarily important in a leader, as long as fairness and judgement prevailed. Popularity, of course, can help but not at the expense of these other qualities. How true that simple wisdom has proved in later years when I have encountered lesser leaders (managers rather than leaders), who obfuscate with detail in order to fudge a decision or end up with an inadequate compromise.

Along with the training establishments and reserve forces, my general's command also encompassed the SBS and I was glad to join him on visits to the unit in Poole and on deployments elsewhere. Firstly, it reunited me with many of those I had trained with and it also allowed me to see the 'bigger picture' of Special Forces deployment. We watched both conventional and counter-terrorism training, including practical demonstrations of SBS tactics to recapture a ship underway in the channel. This sounds straightforward in theory, but add twenty-foot waves, a rolling ship, darkness, the need for stealth, etc. and you get a sense of the huge strength and courage needed simply to get onto the ship – and that is before the assault itself to regain control. Having watched such exercises in practice, we also attended sessions in the government's Cabinet Office Briefing Room (known as COBRA) to coordinate such deployments and it was fascinating to watch the home secretary involved directly in the process. It was a very interesting insight to the SF world and certainly encouraged my thoughts about returning to Poole for a second attempt at the SBS. It was rather fitting, therefore, that my last military parachute jump was with an SBS unit into a fjord in north Norway in mid-winter, chasing our Gemini (inflatable boat) as we leapt from the tailgate of a Hercules. The water, needless to say, was shockingly cold!

Life as an AdC was enjoyably stable and opened my eyes to the more routine world of a desk job and a future beyond soldiering. It also gave me a glimpse of what a steady married life might have delivered had things with Debbie not got derailed. There were summer balls and overseas visits, unit inspections and skiing trips, all of which made for a very pleasant existence. While it was tiring having to explain why I didn't have a South Atlantic medal on my uniform when accompanying Julian on his multiple Falklands presentations, the fact was that I was beginning to pick up the ropes of middle and senior management by osmosis and I became progressively more strategic in my thinking. This proved to be a valuable preparation for my next role, back in the bosom of a commando unit, as adjutant of 42 Commando.

The role of an adjutant is effectively that of the executive officer for the commanding officer. The adjutant implements the instructions of the CO and follows through all the administrative detail. While clearly junior to the second in command and operations officer, as well as the company commanders, the adjutant is critical in the effective running of the commando and his key battle role is running the Command Post, the nerve centre of communications and information. It was a great job to have taken on from my AdC role, especially having listened to Julian's lectures on the Falklands. It was also fascinating to be involved in every detail of what was happening in the commando. I joined just in time to begin pre-Northern Ireland training for a six-month tour in South Armagh where I would run the commando ops room.

It was a good job for me and enabled me to demonstrate my eye for detail and organisational skills. It also marked a clear transition into an executive management role as distinct from a hands-on leadership role and proved to be a valuable lesson for later office life. I was also responsible for discipline in the commando and for keeping the subalterns in check. Since I was only a few months older than some of them, this proved quite challenging at times, but probably only while they tested me out!

The Northern Ireland tour was the normal combination of repetitive and somewhat boring routine, interspersed with some quite intense and dangerous moments. While I was spared the daily patrolling, I was in the ops room monitoring what was happening across the unit 'patch' and ensuring resources and response were coordinated. There are very few incidents to recall other than that, for the first time, I was very conscious of being away from home and my deteriorating relationship with Debbie. It was distracting from what I was doing professionally and I resented it hugely. However, trying to resolve things during an all-too-brief R&R long weekend ended up causing an irreversible breakdown, which marked the beginning of the end of the marriage. I will discuss the issues a bit more later, but having been very careful to always separate the various parts of my life, private and professional, this event crashed through the boundaries and I temporarily struggled to rise above it and keep my focus. In fact, it was a lesson in the realities of life and the insecurities that never lie far from the surface.

Problems with Debbie aside, the tour was very successful, and I remember joining the last patrol out of Crossmaglen (always known as XMG) – notoriously the most volatile area on the border. I remember thinking that if someone doesn't have a go at us, there is no chance of winning an MC! Fortunately, it wasn't one of those moments where you end up regretting what you wished for, as we all returned to base safely. Shortly thereafter, we returned to Bickleigh Barracks for a short holiday before heading off to Norway for our annual three-month Arctic training tour in January. It was a lot of separation from home, but actually the distraction helped and winter warfare was a great new challenge.

Norway in winter is a fairly desolate place with the valleys getting no direct sunshine until mid-March. The landscape appears black and white with virtually no colour and it wasn't surprising to learn that Norway has one of the highest suicide rates in the world. However, as a place to soldier, it was excellent. The weather and environment imposed strict lessons, which you ignored at your peril. I loved it, not least because of the skiing, although military skis were very different to regular alpine skis – as I quickly discovered. The momentum and top-heaviness of a huge rucksack on your back and rifle slung across your chest led to regular and often amusing pile-ups. We spent several days at a time out in the mountains and developed an incredible closeness to nature. Watching the Aurora Borealis at 3am while on sentry duty is an ethereal experience, and the beauty and peace of the mountains was truly serene. Skiing at night wasn't quite so ethereal, however, as it proved very difficult to judge a gradient, leading to some spectacular crashes into trees, unexpected drops and massive snow drifts! But militarily we found we could operate extremely effectively living in bivouac shelters or snow holes, and it was amazing how much distance could be covered over difficult terrain by a proficient troop. This was classic Royal Marines territory where teamwork, fitness, endurance, and our amphibious capability came into its own.

After completing my arctic warfare course, I reluctantly headed back to commando headquarters to resume my adjutant roles, but I would head out on patrol as often as I got the chance. Once again, my key task was to manage the Command Post and in the Arctic, we used Volvo BV over-snow vehicles. It immediately took me back to my BAOR time in armoured personnel carriers and I was able to construct a totally new set-up for the BVs based on the BAOR model. Our CP became the most efficient in the Brigade as a result and the brigade major, ironically my old course officer from training, instructed the other units to copy my set-up. It is fun to look back on those pre-computer days and remember how primitive it was when we had such basic coding tools (to encode or decode a grid reference, for example) or, much worse, when we completed amphibious loading tables by hand. The latter was rather like doing an old-fashioned puzzle; you had to work out the order in which you wanted everyone to arrive on land and then reverse all the elements, including any cross-decking from other ships, so that everyone and everything arrived in the right place at the right time with the right kit. After all, you don't want your supply wagons arriving before the assault troops or leave the back half of a gun team in the wrong landing craft. It was an intellectual challenge, but hugely rewarding to get it right first go.

We returned to Bickleigh in Easter 1985 and there was a change of COs, which provided me with important handover and continuity responsibilities. The new CO had commanded the SBS when I did my course and perhaps because he had got to know me then and the mutual respect that goes with anyone who has been involved in Special Forces work, we got along really well. We had many conversations about whether I should return and take the course again, and he strongly urged me to do so. But the intervening years had opened my eyes to other interests, both military and social, and it wasn't such an obvious decision as before. I mulled it over for about six months, but concluded that I wanted to re-establish a home life ahead of heading back into a specialised military role. I think it was the right decision at that stage.

The immediate goal was a short commitment on public duties in London, guarding the royal palaces and the Tower of London. We spent ages brushing up our drill and it proved to be an excellent and very different challenge for all of us. We were thrust into the public eye and became the first soldiers on parade at Buckingham Palace with the new rifle, the SA 80, as the old and redoubtable SLR was phased out. It was a chance to show off and put on a swagger and I found that as Captain of the Queen's Guard, I had several privileges – one of which was hosting lunch and dinner parties at St James's Palace. What a great invitation this proved with the girls! I managed to repay all sorts of old debts and establish plenty more contacts, which was especially gratifying in my new life as a single man again. I also had the honour to be presented to the Queen and the Duke of Edinburgh at a private audition in the palace during a visit by the president of Germany. There were a host of special rules that had to be followed about what to do or not do at any particular moment and I recall with amusement one incident that could have ended tragically, but for the reaction of the local police constable (PC) on the gate of the palace. I remember being told that officers on guard should never look right or left before crossing the traffic as the traffic should always give way to the Queen's Guard Commander! Well, that was all well and good when you are wearing a bright red Guards uniform as cars had a better chance of seeing you! I mercifully avoided being run down as the duty PC leapt out into the traffic to halt a particularly determined minivan from mowing me down! But that apart, a stint of duty in London was a real tonic and classic 'chocolate-box soldiering', although I'm glad I never joined the Guards.

Back to Lympstone

All too soon and after some challenging exercises, my two years at 42 Commando was up. My next appointment was back to the Commando Training Centre at Lympstone where I was to join the Officers' Training Wing. In fact, I was grateful for this as I wanted to develop my training skills and teaching officers was always regarded as the pinnacle. It also coincided with the start of the ill-fated course that Prince Edward joined. Although I wasn't his course officer, I could see that he was a fish out of water and lacked a close 'buddy' to help him through the bad days. But I also think the Corps could have done more to ensure that he completed training, so he could have taken his part as a royal in subsequent public events. But the Corps decided that he should be given no favours and, as a result, he flunked it. It was sad for him on a personal level. Since I taught tactics, he never got as far as my modules as he had dropped out at the end of basic Phase 1 training. Having been his escort at the 1977 Silver Jubilee event in Plymouth ten years earlier, it would have been nice to have seen him progress into adult life with a credible RM role.

My return to Lympstone coincided with a period of reflection on where my career in the Royal Marines might go and what other alternatives to a military life there might be. Apart from my premature attempt to join the SBS and develop a career within the Special Forces, I had done most of the jobs I wanted to do and had commanded at troop level for far longer than most. The next rung of the ladder would have been company commander and then the whole progression through staff college and senior command. The prospects of an interesting military career seemed rather limited back in 1986. The Russians clearly weren't going to roll across the central plains of Germany, nor seize the Norwegian fjords for their submarines, and frankly I didn't want to spend another six months (or more) in Northern Ireland trying to win an unwinnable war. The prospect was just more of the same, and having missed the Falklands conflict and the chance to test my mettle for real, I began to get restless. How ironic it was that less than three years later, the Soviet Union collapsed, leading to a dismantling of the 'Wall' across Europe and an upsurge in nationalistic struggles across the Balkans and elsewhere. Not to mention a few years later, two Gulf wars and then Afghanistan, all of which placed a reliance on military options that we hadn't seen for a generation. It became a much more interesting military environment, although, unquestioningly, a more dangerous one.

But without the benefit of a crystal ball, there were also two other elements to my restlessness, the first being Carol, who entered my life on 30th July that year and opened my eyes to a wider world and the opportunities beyond. The second was a progressively debilitating back injury, which eventually narrowed down to a historic compression fracture of L4 and L5, probably caused by a combination of skiing accidents (one in particular during a downhill race in Val d'Isère), one or two poor parachute landings, and the colossal and awkward weights I carried on the SBS course.

My role as an instructor was to instil the essential qualities needed of a commando officer in a new generation of young men. However, it also created an inner contradiction I found troubling. I enjoyed motivating and inspiring these young men and I created some challenging and realistic tactical exercises that tested my own professional skills. But deep down, I had turned a corner and realised it was time to move on. I also saw the next stages of my career as being desk-bound and rather less interesting, even though the opportunities at senior command level – which I rather arrogantly assumed I would achieve – would have been more exciting. I was not alone in this career dilemma as several of my contemporaries were reflecting on their own options in exactly the same way, and it often appeared to be the ablest that were leaving as they had the initiative and entrepreneurial drive to try something different. That is not to say that those that stayed were laggards, but a lot of talented officers were leaving at exactly my stage (turning thirty, getting married and feeling depressed by the prospects of military life in an inactive 'Cold War' environment) and if we didn't leave when we did, we would get tied in by staff college commitments and the 'return of service' obligations that ensued.

Looking back over my time in the Corps, I realise it was the making of me and prepared me for the next phase of my life better than any university or life coach could possibly have done. I had pushed myself and achieved far more than I thought possible. I had developed a strong sense of duty and a personal commitment to maintaining the highest of standards and, above all, I had had fun doing it. Fun isn't a very professional word, but it is so important in life and all the more so in today's ultra-serious world. I have never regretted any moment of my RM career and remain hugely proud of the traditions and excellence that continue. If there is any regret, it is more a curiosity of wondering how far up the ladder I would have climbed and, given the dangers that emerged in subsequent wars, how well I would have performed. Something for bath-time reflection and no more!

So, after some twelve and a half years' commissioned service, I 'hung up my boots' and accepted a medical discharge, which I qualified for as a result of my back injuries and hearing loss, and headed out into the future, wondering what life would bring.

Receiving my green beret from Colonel David Bailey – March 1976

Pass-out parade at Lympstone, en route to 42 Commando – July 1976

1975 Young Officer group photo. NB My great friend, Clive Richards, second row, third from left.

The Royal Marines under-19 rugby squad – 1975

Escort to Prince Edward at the Queen's Silver Jubilee parade – 1977

With Prince Andrew and Prince Edward in the jungle stance – 1977

K Company 42 Commando in Vieques, Virgin Islands – 1977

On patrol in Belfast – 1978

A burnt-out bus on the Falls Road, Belfast – 1978

En route to RM Poole for SBS training – 1978

The dreaded balloon jump

Post-mud run on SBS course – 1978

King's Squad pass out with HRH Prince Philip 1979

Sitting on a captured Russian T62
tank in Werl – 1979

Inner German Border patrol – 1980

The Inner German Border – 1980

Jungle training in Belize – 1980

In mess kit while serving as AdC to General Thompson

Arctic warfare training, Norway – 1985

The Commando CP on exercise in Norway – 1985

42 Commando officers at Lom, Norway – 1986

Captain of the Queen's Guard,
Buckingham Palace – 1986

*Changing the Guard ceremony at
Buckingham Palace – 1986*

On Woodbury Common, Lympstone – 1987

Chapter Four

Love

It has been strange writing about the first thirty years of my life without really having addressed the whole subject of girls, love and my approach to relationships. It would have made the earlier chapters rather complicated, hence why I will attempt to condense into one chapter the rather bumpy path I have followed in the pursuit of girls, happiness, love, general curiosity and often just the thrill of the chase.

The combination of a rather insular home life and single-sex schooling meant that until my last year at Eton, girls were a genuine novelty for me in any personal or emotional sense, let alone physically. If you add to that the general sexual permissiveness of the 1970s and the naturally high testosterone levels of a red-blooded seventeen-year-old boy, the chances of me getting it all wrong were very high! Being 'locked up' in another all-male environment in the Royal Marines only made it worse.

Of course, at the time I thought everything was fine and the excitement of discovering that a girl other than a relative was interested in me was a huge rush. So having dealt with the awkwardness of virginity with a kindly woman in Soho, I set about finding a girlfriend (NB: before any old girlfriends start to get sweaty palms, this is not a 'kiss-and-tell' exposé and only those who were involved will recognise the circumstances of certain stories).

On reflection, my instincts were rather selfish, but I never started out with any intention of being uncaring, indeed, I considered myself to be very sensitive and understanding (as long as things turned out my way). It is just that I felt I had to make up for years of lost time and that I needed to cram as many experiences into my life as quickly as possible. What fun it was and mostly achieved with mutual enjoyment and/or without recriminations. Of course, in the pre-social media world of the '70s, there was a more liberal approach to friendships – at least that's the way it appeared and, certainly, there was no danger of having compromising photos emailed around the world. I realise that such duplicity sounds shocking now, but, in fact, it worked both ways. The 'relationship' tags of today, where everyone publishes partner status with 'claims' staked out rather like land-markers in the nineteenth century US, seem only to tie people together prematurely, when, in fact, what individuals need in their twenties is freedom.

Girlfriends – or, perhaps more accurately, friends who were girls – started off being limited to those who were daughters of our parents' friends. They were normally introduced as being "such a nice girl… so clever… and with lovely parents". The fact that there might be zero chemistry, were ugly and/or have no discernible graces, somehow failed to register at parent level. Accordingly, I was obliged to look further afield where, very often, the girls who I wanted to spend some time with had few of the virtues apparently so important to parents. Hence, in the early days, I brought very few of them home. Subconsciously I was making a distinction between 'parentally suitable' girls – that is to say, those with a similar background, interests, education, values, etc – and girls who wanted to have fun. For a long time, I assumed that such virtues were mutually exclusive and heading off into the Royal Marines just meant that such compartmentalisation continued. I only realise looking back that, of course, a vital part of the emotional maturing process can happen at university, where like-minded relationships can develop more naturally. My emotional maturing process happened in the Royal Marines, surrounded by other hormonally exuberant men! Is it surprising it took a bit longer for some lessons to register?

Whether by luck or good judgement (luck, almost certainly), I did meet some incredibly nice girls, and the house parties and long weekend trips around the country after leaving Eton were filled more with laughter and teenage pranks than sexual indulgence. Life was still remarkably innocent and I wasn't in the hippy or drug scene, so was very naïve about how slippery the slope could be for teenagers at that time. I was happy to have lots of friends who were girls and had no interest in becoming too serious with anyone in particular. Life didn't change much in the early days at Lympstone either as we were always too busy or away on exercise. I looked for safety in numbers at the first officers' mess Christmas party, inviting two girls down from home, only to get caught kissing someone else on the dance floor to the sound of Procol Harem's *A Whiter Shade of Pale* – not very clever!

Social life didn't really pick up until I left Lympstone and headed out to Bickleigh with 42 Commando. There were some wonderful pubs around the edge of Dartmoor and we got to know many of the local drinking holes, such as the 'Who'd have Thought It' in Milton Coombe, the 'Plume of Feathers' in Princeton and the 'Peter Tavy Inn' in – guess where – Peter Tavy! For visiting girlfriends, these were wonderfully charismatic places, totally different to the London pubs of the time and arriving in my open-top Triumph Spitfire in the depth of winter would always get the blood going. The challenge in Devon at the time was that most self-respecting girls our age wanted to be somewhere else, such as London or Oxford or even Exeter, where there was more going on. So, we young officers had to resort to the local dives in Plymouth for entertainment, where it was highly improbable that we would meet any girls with whom we might want to develop a broader relationship. Indeed, there was a rather unedifying mess tradition of awarding a trophy to the officer who managed to bring home the least attractive girl for a drink at the mess. Hardly a culture likely to encourage a mature approach to the opposite sex!

There were two main venues in Plymouth where we officers would go, one rather better than the other. The first was officially called the Plymouth Sailing Club, but more normally known as the 'GX' (short for the Groin Exchange), which makes it sound more disreputable than it was. It was based in one of the old wharf buildings alongside Plymouth Barbican in the old port and the atmosphere was quite cool by 1970s standards. There was a very good disco that played great music and it wasn't so loud that you couldn't speak to each other, which allowed you to check that your prospective partner for the evening could at least string a few sentences together. The other place was the Fiesta Club on Union Street. This had rather less going for it. It was also directly opposite 'Diamond Lil's' strip club, which meant it would often get overrun by drunken sailors… followed by the shore patrol. We used to limit our visits to Thursdays, which were known as 'Granny night' as you were supposed to be over twenty-one to get in! The music was dire and very loud and there would typically be several groups of girls on the dance floor, dancing around their handbags, while the men all stood on the edge making disparaging comments and deciding who to approach. Off the dance floor, the biggest challenge was avoiding getting stuck to the beer-soaked carpet. In fact, I can't remember what we saw in the place other than as a chance to try out our chat-up lines! It really was a different age.

One episode in 1979 was a bit of a watershed in my overly casual approach to girls. I wish I could say that it changed me, but it took a few more instances of brazen self-centeredness before I realised that I was genuinely upsetting others with my behaviour. I now refer to this as the Exeter St David's Station incident. The background was, of course, completely innocent. My recruit troop were due to be passed for duty by Prince Philip and, months ahead of the date, all those involved were asked to submit names of wives and girlfriends for the lunch afterwards. As I had no girlfriend at the time, I asked a friend from home to be my partner. Anyway, between inviting this girl (let's call her 'A') and the date of the parade, I met a really lovely girl ('B') from Exeter University for whom I had developed some genuine feelings. B and I became inseparable as the date of the parade neared and I realised that I had a crisis brewing when B said she would like to stay on an extra week after the end of university term to be with me. This then became eight days, then nine and, before I knew it, she was due to depart home on the same day as A was due to arrive. There was no way I was going to be able to wriggle my way out of this one and it was literally an impending train wreck. I knew one or other relationship was going to get toasted. It was a teary and very unhappy moment as I confessed to B and I would not encourage any aspiring lover to try and finesse their luck in this way. It says a great deal about B that, despite this dreadful incident, we have remained dear friends to this day. She even asked me to speak on her behalf at her wedding and I haven't seen or heard from A in over forty years!

Relationships continued to be rather short-lived affairs and living with Clive in 1978 in his house in Exmouth probably marked the low point in our respective understanding of the opposite sex. Apart from a rather enjoyable camping holiday with two girls in the South of France, I otherwise struggled to find anyone who was prepared to be abandoned whenever I went off on exercise or was on duty. From 1979 onwards, however, I found that my best chance to meet an interesting and broader mix of girls was in the Alps. At that time, I was spending up to six weeks a year skiing with the Royal Navy ski team in places like Val d'Isère, St Anton, Les Arcs, etc. and the holiday atmosphere, albeit technically I was on duty, provided a relaxed environment in which to meet girls. It was also a million miles away from the dreary life of Plymouth, Portsmouth or various other garrison towns and dockyards in which I normally found myself.

I met 'C' during a snowball fight in Tignes and she became my first regular girlfriend; that is to say, our relationship lasted more than the normal two to three weeks. In fact, we went out, on and off, for nearly three years and became very fond of each other, notwithstanding her fierce temper and outspokenness, which, of course, was quite endearing. She managed to get herself fired from the hotel in which she was working and I recall one dreadfully long night as we walked, with all her luggage, from Tignes to Val d'Isère (through the unlit tunnels), arriving into Val at about 6am. It was a test of character (clearly not of common sense) and we sort of bonded after that. She was less forgiving when I nearly drove her off a cliff in my old VW beetle, which hit a patch of ice and rolled onto its side off a snow bank, inches from a 200-foot drop into the Tignes reservoir. She was even less impressed when I asked her not to get out first, lest the car roll onto its roof and damage my race skis. Some of her suggestions for what I could do with my skis were impractical anyway!

That aside, we had plenty of funny moments. Late one evening, a gang of us left a nightclub in Val d'Isère and decided to go for a swim in the outside pool of one of the smart hotels. We climbed over the fence, stripped off and jumped in. The pool was covered in ping pong balls and was lovely and warm and we tried to encourage the others to follow. But they had other ideas and stole our clothes, leaving just our moon boots, and then raced back to the apartment. C and I climbed out, into the sub-zero night air, stark naked and wet, and chased after them. Needless to say, we attracted hoots of laughter and snowballs from passers-by. When we arrived in our apartment building on the other side of the town centre, we were freezing! We got into the lift for our flat on the 4th floor, but the lift stopped on the 3rd floor where a gaggle of people were waiting to get in. Since we were both so wet and cold, there wasn't much to see, but it was one of those moments where you really have nothing to say. It made for a good story and for payback later.

I was serving with the Queen's Regiment at the time and after the ski season, I drove C up to Germany where she lived, unofficially, in the mess with me for about three weeks. Since this was supposed to be single-sex accommodation, it was quite a feat to remain undetected, although I suspect that, in fact, everyone did know. One morning, on the Battalion's main ceremonial day, Albuhera Day, marking a historic battle during the Peninsular War, the tradition, unknown to me, was to wake officers with a stirring bugle and drums call through the mess. As the drummers progressed down the corridor towards my room, I looked around at the blizzard of female clothes, underwear, etc. lying all over the place and realised that I had no chance to tidy it all up. I just pushed C under the bedcovers in the small single bed and hoped for the best. The drummers must have been primed as they didn't come in and I was never held to account. She became something of a mascot for the subalterns thereafter, being whisked out of trouble by plenty of willing accomplices.

It was still a very false existence in terms of what building a steady relationship meant, with no chance for any stable time together. Deployments were non-stop and social life had to fit into the very limited time left over. So, we reverted to 'hunter killer' sorties to the local towns in search of entertainment, apparently having learned very little from previous experiences. It was to be the next ski season before a new clutch of love affairs started, one being on the very first day in the Alps. The Royal Navy (RN) squad had just arrived in Valloire, a quiet French resort off the Maurienne Valley, where there was some excellent snow and good skiing. On the first day, I saw a very pretty girl about to get on the long chair lift up from the town, alone, which seemed a terrible wasted opportunity. I crashed over several sets of skis and people to jump on next to her and had secured a date before we reached the top. 'D' was French, spoke little English and was a pacifist. It was a challenge but we ended up hitting it off. She was very lively and we got immersed in the local French life, which was a great change. She was also very fit and we later won the annual cross-country race around town (fastest boy and fastest girl), which earned us dinner together in the best restaurant.

Having promised D that I was different from other boys and wouldn't just head straight into the arms of another girl when I moved on to Val d'Isère after the two weeks in Valloire, this is, in fact, exactly what happened. Once again, on the first day in the resort (early January 1981), I bumped straight into a very pretty English / Swiss girl. Her name was Debbie (one of only two girls I will name, for reasons that will become clear in due course). Debbie's parents were both English, but she was brought up in

Geneva and, to all intents and purposes, was Swiss. She was only twenty when I met her and a runway model for some of the Swiss fashion houses. She was striking and unusual and quite exotic, qualities I found intoxicating and I fell for her immediately. Slightly unusually, my parents were in the Alps to watch me race in the British Championships and so this early courtship was conducted largely under their gaze. Somehow, it lent a bit more legitimacy to our budding friendship and Debbie seemed as smitten as I was. After the racing in Val, we moved on to Les Arcs for some FIS races and then Ischgl in Austria for the army championships, before heading back to Valloire for the inter-services. I slightly dreaded the return to Valloire where I knew D would be waiting and it was not a good moment. I was, at least, quite practised at wriggling out of relationships by that point!

Debbie was unusual in many ways, but she made it clear very quickly that she was prepared to fit her life around mine rather than the other way around. Given that military life was so peripatetic, this was massively important to me and gave me hope that I could continue with my active military career while also developing an emotional base, something which was blatantly missing in my life. I was also undeniably attracted to her on a physical level and enjoyed her 'head-turning' qualities, which I knew would be admired back at home. How superficial this sounds now, yet it seemed so important at the time, and I was so distracted both by this and her behaviour towards me that I failed to consider other far more important questions, such as whether we were both mature enough to enter such a relationship and whether we had the same values and interests, along with multiple other considerations.

But it was certainly an intense start to our relationship. We spent almost ten weeks together non-stop and that intensity then continued by mail once I returned to sunny Belize (where I was serving with the Queen's Regiment). In fact, it even picked up, if that were possible. Absence definitely did make the heart grow fonder! By the time I returned to Europe, I had decided that I wanted to marry her and, while enjoying some spring skiing in Zermatt, I proposed and she accepted. From Zermatt, we drove down the Simplon Pass to Venice and had one of the most romantic weekends possible. At this point, I had known her for just under four months and had been with her less than half that time.

The rest of 1981 was a bit of a blur as we prepared for the wedding. I was travelling around the country on a recruiting job and Debbie found a job at Gatwick Airport, where she seemed to spend all her time dealing with irate (or idiotic) passengers. Not a happy job! But the wedding on 19th December in Wimborne Minster (which is where Sue and her husband, Frank, lived), followed by a reception in the Officers' Mess at Poole, was very special. We headed off to Tunisia for a quick week's honeymoon before flying to the Alps for the start of ski training with the Navy. Those first few weeks were intensely happy and I thought I was the luckiest man alive.

Tragedy struck less than eight weeks after the wedding when Debbie's mother died after a very rapid decline with cancer. We knew she had been ill, but she had hidden the extent of it during our engagement and I am sure she was just holding on in order to see us marry. Poor Debbie and her father were inconsolable. I had never experienced such grief and found it very difficult to handle. The months went by and she was still crying herself to sleep or breaking down for no apparent reason. I had just taken up a new role as AdC to the general in Portsmouth and I found Debbie's emotional isolation and lack of intimacy harder and harder to understand. It created a wedge between us, which only ever seemed to get wider, leading to misunderstandings and arguments. On top of everything, I was dealing with the overpowering disappointment of missing the Falklands deployment in May 1982.

After about a year, we sought out help from marriage guidance and from my dear Aunt Mary (Mum's sister), who was a professional counsellor in Cambridge. For a short period, things seemed to get a better. We had a holiday in Greece in the summer of 1983, which was probably the nearest we returned to the happy days of old, and I began to hope that we might be beginning to re-establish normality. But events were not helpful as, in early 1984, I was posted to Plymouth as adjutant of 42 Commando to prepare for our Northern Ireland tour. The fourteen-month separation that followed with pre-deployment training, the tour itself and then three months' arctic training in Norway in early 1985 proved fatal. Debbie found solace with someone else while I was away (unbeknownst to me at the time) and her demeanour towards me cooled dramatically and frighteningly. The realisation that I was losing her was overwhelming. I was consumed with self-pity; with guilt for my selfishness in wanting everything my way; for failing to be sufficiently understanding of her grief; and anything else I could pile on. It was undoubtedly the worst six-month period of my life. Never have expressions such as 'wanting space' sounded so painful, and it was only the discovery of the other man that allowed me finally to focus my sadness and frustration away from myself and begin to move forwards. The divorce was relatively simple, as we had few assets, and we closed the chapter on our marriage in June 1986 after four and a half years. I was left with the large house in Portland Road, Plymouth, and not much else. I had to sell my prized Lancia Montecarlo sports car and I reverted to another trusty old VW beetle, which I bought for £300. Since I could barely cook (some things never change), at least I had the option to eat at the mess, which became a lifesaver.

So what do I make of this episode in my life, looking back after thirty-five years? Probably the most important realisation at the time was that I had been emotionally selfish and that while I had expected Debbie to give her all to me, I could somehow be more selective in what I gave back. I also now realise that I had been role-playing rather than living life for real. I had fallen in love with the idea of being married to a beautiful girl, rather than actually being in love with the girl herself. It was hardly surprising that I hadn't been able to engage with her grief or recognise her needs. I also felt that I had failed; failed in a relationship and failed to deliver on my wedding promises. Divorce was still stigmatised in the 1980s and certainly in the forces, and somehow it all seemed very un-Christian, even though I hardly qualified as a good Christian. But as the pain slowly subsided and those irritating people stopped telling me about 'other pebbles on the beach', I realised that I was lucky to have shared this short marriage with Debbie. There were no children involved and we had both matured enormously through our experiences together. Importantly, we were lucky to have been able to end it when we did and rebuild our lives separately with youth and energy on our sides.

I also made one other important discovery, although not immediately. It was that saying goodbye to someone you love, whether for a few days or several months, was going to become harder and harder to do. I even wonder if this wasn't rooted in some of those teary goodbyes from Marlborough House School days. But, undoubtedly, it began to manifest itself in some of my later decisions, such as turning down the opportunity to return to SBS training and also, eventually, the decision to leave the Royal Marines altogether. Perhaps I was finally growing up!

Being back in the singles world felt a bit odd at first, but rapidly picked up. I became rather more selective in my taste and knew that I wanted companionship as much as anything else, which meant interaction on both an intellectual and cultural level rather than simply conquest! It was no longer an unspoken competition, but rather a desire to find a soulmate and herein lay the same dilemma I had faced before with being stuck in the West Country. I don't mean to suggest that there aren't lots of wonderful girls there, but I had developed a more international outlook and friends and I found many British girls frighteningly introspective and dull. The answer was to head to London and I reconnected with B and C, with a view to meeting a new circle of friends. I travelled to London almost every weekend, camping on sofas wherever I could, and quickly realised that as a young Royal Marines officer, I was rather different to the normal banker, broker or estate agent that was hanging around London pubs. However, it also reinforced my emotional loneliness and I knew that I needed a spot of luck.

Skiing came to the rescue with a combined services trip to Australia. This was a special opportunity and representing the UK services was exciting, let alone the trip to Oz. After an incredibly long trip in an RAF VC10 via Germany, Sri Lanka, Singapore and Darwin, we finally arrived in Sydney in torrential rain in early July 1986, nearly thirty-six hours later. We then almost immediately headed off to the Snowy Mountain resort of Thredbo, a further four-hour minivan trip.

On arrival, the only thing we wanted was a strong drink and, by coincidence, we found ourselves with a bunch of girls who had also just arrived from Sydney and had the same idea. Well, one thing led to another and I soon became ensconced with one of them, 'E', and things developed from there. It was a wild and boozy time in true Oz style and we all had enormous fun, carrying on the party in Sydney for a few days after the skiing ended. It was the perfect tonic to what had been a difficult year to date and was a great personal boost for me. I also experienced one of those moments when, contrary to popular myth, I felt genuinely intimidated waking up in a room with five other girls – and didn't they just know it! The trip home from Australia wasn't quite so tedious, but I was already suffering withdrawal symptoms from E and wondering how I could possibly maintain a relationship from the other side of the world. The telephone bill alone was going to be impossible. Little did I know how irrelevant all this would be only a few days later.

Before heading 'down under', I had agreed to attend a fundraising bash for the Duke of Edinburgh's Awards at a friend's rather grand stately home in Oxfordshire. He and I had met during RN ski training and he had married the sister of an old school friend of mine, so we had lots of friends in common, but from a much wider cross section than normal RN or RM life. The event had been organised as a day of competitions from tennis, croquet, clay pigeon shooting, etc. and we were all divided up into teams. I was asked to be team captain of my group and I found a rather pretty American girl, Carol, had been assigned to my team. She was wearing a bright red sweater and red jeans, and had a special shyness about her that was intriguing. She was also incredibly competitive, I discovered, although completely hopeless at tennis, croquet, ping pong and, indeed, anything involving a ball. However, we discovered that we made a good team at the piggyback race and, more interestingly, the double sack race. The latter involving very active and coordinated jumping together in the sack. Well, you can see where this is headed! As Mark enjoyed saying as my best man at our wedding in New York two years later, Carol and I met in the sack and never really looked back.

The immediate follow-up to our meeting in Oxfordshire wasn't exactly propitious as I lost Carol's number and found I had given her the wrong number for my house in Plymouth. So, I was relieved to receive a call through the operator at the Commando Training Centre where she had tracked me down. Well, this, in itself, was a good sign. We agreed to meet for dinner in London the following week when I knew I needed to be in town for the RN dry skiing championships at the Hillingdon ski centre. I found myself strangely nervous but also excited as I drove up to town in my battered old grey VW beetle. I parked next to her very smart blue BMW M3 in Lowndes Street, which curiously had a German number plate, and knocked on her door. It was the start of an interesting evening, which I learned later had been orchestrated by Carol around me. Strangely, there were four of us called Richard sitting around the table that night, which made for some confusion. But the guest who made the biggest impression on me was Carol's old friend, Caroline. After the other guests had left, she and Carol grilled me on everything: background, career, likes/dislikes and, of course, why I had got divorced. Caroline was asking all the questions, but I was really answering for Carol, who sat in the edge of her seat trying not to look too interested. I left after 2am, hoping I had done OK!

The next day, I headed out to Hillingdon for the ski competition. It was a low-key event but I expected to do quite well and so I was both surprised and pleased when Carol turned up to watch. Well, I thought I would be able to impress her with my skill, if nothing else. Tragically, I achieved exactly the opposite, crashing out of the course at the bottom and smashing my knee against a metal stanchion. While I was waiting for the ambulance to take me off to Uxbridge A&E, I was really touched by how genuinely concerned Carol was. She could also see that I was very uncomfortable sitting on a backless bench and moved next to me so I could lean against her. It was a small but incredibly touching gesture, which I remember to this day, and I heard, very clearly, an inner voice saying to me: 'Here is a very special person – take note and don't screw it up.'

Carol went to hospital with me and then took me back to her flat where she looked after me for the weekend. They were possibly some of the loveliest few days I can remember, where companionship, comfort and a sense of certainty of purpose overtook both of us. Any nervousness I may have had about exposing myself emotionally to someone again disappeared that weekend and I found it impossible to think about anyone else. All this was happening less than six months after my divorce was finalised with Debbie and was the last thing I expected. For a few fleeting moments, I regretted that the carefree existence I had resumed was to be cut short so quickly. But there was a depth to my appreciation and feelings for Carol, which was unlike anything I had felt before and, furthermore, it was being reflected in a truly wonderful way. I still so vividly remember feeling Carol's heart thumping though her chest when we were close and it was a voyage of intense self-discovery as we realised that we were falling in love with each other. If this was what true love felt like, then I certainly had never been in love before.

Carol also brought a whole new dimension and perspective to my life. Firstly, she was American – actually, half American and half South African – and while meeting foreign girls wasn't new in itself, she had a sophistication and poise that was different from anyone I had met before. Secondly, she lived in London, travelled extensively, went hunting regularly in Leicestershire and generally led a very independent existence, all of which was a million miles from the life I led in the Royal Marines. Thirdly, she didn't appear to need to work to support all these activities and so could follow her whims and instincts without the normal constraints. Indeed, it was this encouragement to think 'outside the box' and not let circumstances dictate that was to prove so valuable to me in the years ahead. I had no idea until much later that this independent lifestyle was possible because of the success of the Maytag Corporation, a US white goods manufacturer (washing machines and fridges etc.) set up by her great grandfather, from which she had inherited a trust. Mind you, while this sounds great, the assumptions it triggered in people who found out about this were always very predictable.

In a strange way, my discovery that she was quite wealthy made me all the more determined not to rely on her financially as I didn't want anyone to think that this is what was motivating me. However, I can't deny it was a wonderful surprise and underwrote a lot of the risk in decisions we subsequently took together.

There were hardly enough hours in the day to contain our excitement and the momentum of our relationship picked up rapidly. Since I was still training officers at Lympstone, it meant that most weekends were spent travelling up to London or hosting Carol in Devon. I had rented a small thatched cottage in a village on the edge of Woodbury Common and this was a beautiful and romantic bolthole. My first visit to New York in the summer of 1987 gave me a better understanding of Carol's childhood and background, which was quite challenging in many respects, while privileged in others. Her mother, Shirley, clearly saw me as an outsider, which made for some interesting moments, but she had a great sense of humour and I used this to defuse difficult occasions. Carol's family had endured its share of tragedy. Her father, Bob Maytag, had died when she was six and her stepfather, Kerryn King, died in 1986, just after we had met in England. If this wasn't enough, her brother, Christopher, died very unexpectedly in early 1987. It was a tragic backdrop to what should have been a gilded family life and I am very sad that I never met any of these men. However, helping Shirley close up Christopher's house in Florida after his death was a chance to build bridges and to learn more about what made this family tick.

As an aside, on that first trip to Orlando, Carol and I decided to go water-skiing on one of the big lakes nearby. It was really just an excuse for me to show off as normal and we covered the length and breadth of the lake. It was only after we came home that we were informed that the lake was notorious for alligators, who loved all the little coves and creeks where we had been swimming and/or waiting to restart after a fall! I flinch just thinking about it now.

I proposed to Carol on Woodbury Common in Devon one sunny summer lunchtime in 1987. The picture of me in uniform that day sits on our landing table at home and captures that special moment. It is hard to describe how special it felt to hear her say, "Yes", even though I half knew she would accept. The journey from that day to the wedding on 28th May 1988 went by in a flash. Part of me was nervous about going through the formalities and repeating the vows I made to Debbie only seven years earlier, but as I got closer to the day, I realised that this was completely different. This was the real thing. I knew that this was love and my declarations, therefore, had profoundly more meaning. In fact, the actual moment of having to make them saw me choked with emotion so that my words were almost inaudible to all but those immediately around the altar. The whole wedding weekend in New York was an incredible memory. The pre-wedding boat party around Manhattan, the service in St Thomas's on Fifth Avenue and then the afternoon and dinner receptions at the Metropolitan Club were spectacular. In fact, it would be impossible to have achieved a more spectacular start to our married life.

Our honeymoon in the Seychelles, Mauritius and South Africa was the most wonderful escape from reality and a chance to savour the excitement and introspection of new love. We had the most amazing holiday and those carefree days of mutual self-discovery and companionship were priceless. Looking back at the photos of us looking so young and innocent still bring back the sights, smells and sounds of Africa and everything that is so special about those first few days of married life.

This chapter isn't about telling the story of married life; so I will spend a few moments trying to distil what I have learned over the last thirty plus years with Carol and how our love has matured and deepened over this time. The films would have you believe that young couples walk off into the sunset hand in hand and 'live happily ever after'. Well, I am glad (and relieved) to say that Carol and I have enjoyed a wonderfully full and rewarding life together so far, but feelings aren't static, and love needs to evolve to stay real and fulfilling. As things have turned out, I think we have had far fewer challenges than many young couples and I think we can both be proud of this. But there are always issues that bubble up from time to time and complacency is the greatest threat to stability and trust. One of the first things I learned with Debbie is that passion and love are not the same thing and it is easy to confuse one with the other. Equally, the absence of one need not preclude the other. For me, passion is that convergence of emotions and energy that creates an almost blind desire to be with another person and, undoubtedly, this is the driving force behind the early days of meeting someone and getting to know them. But maintaining that tempo is unusual and normally unrealistic – a fact that can then often surprise and disappoint those without deeper bonds of love and understanding to support them in a longer relationship.

The true foundation of love and indeed any long-term relationship, however, is trust. It is the unspoken 'sine qua non' that couples take for granted until something goes wrong. However, trust isn't a static concept any more than love itself and it needs to accommodate the natural changes that take place in a relationship over time. The most critical part of trust is the mutual desire to be respected and loved. Kindness is a key part of this and I recall asking both future sons-in-law to promise me that they would always be kind to my daughters whatever the circumstances and whatever their feelings. I hope I have been mostly kind to Carol, despite testing her patience by being incurably flirtatious and easily distracted by pretty girls. She has always understood that this was only superficial and I have equally maintained that it has reinforced my happiness (and reminded me of my good fortune) in being married to Carol.

One thing I have learned, however, is that putting oneself in temptation's way is dangerous, and you need to take a conscious decision to avoid getting caught up in a situation where things could get out of hand. I have always been a subscriber to the 'cock up rather than conspiracy' theory of life. Circumstances are what normally conspire to trip us up rather than conscious intentions and the key is to stay alert to that change in atmosphere when the mood of a moment changes from innocent fun to something more. No truer is this than during the so-called midlife crisis. Contrary to myth, this doesn't happen in one's midlife, but much later – in my case, my mid-fifties. I mark it as that moment when, despite sucking your tummy in and trying to pluck out the grey hairs, you realise you are getting older and the pretty girls are no longer looking at you! Since we are all pre-programmed to be wanted and desired, the dangers of temptation take on new meaning at this volatile stage in life, and it can be all too sad to see couples coming unstuck and recklessly jettisoning twenty or thirty years of married life for the excitement of something new. As I have said, passion can be a dangerous emotion to contain or understand, making one blind to the reality of what is at stake. I count myself lucky for just avoiding being cast onto the rocks by those siren calls, for Carol's forgiveness and understanding, and the realisation that our love had never disappeared in the first place.

Of course, this chapter remains open-ended, but if I have learned nothing else over the last thirty years, it is that happiness and emotional security are easy to take for granted yet are the fundamental ingredients for long-term fulfilment. Carol has needed the patience of a saint dealing with me over the last thirty years, but I also know that our time together has been mutually enriching and, corny as it may sound, she and I are soulmates. So, the prospects of another twenty to thirty years together look good if I can stay out of trouble!

Party time – c1979

*Wedding reception with Debbie –
19th December 1981*

Debbie – 1981

Misbehaving,
Thredbo, Australia
– 1986

At a county fair – c1987

Carol – 1987

*Carol's engagement
photo – 1987*

*Our wedding at the Metropolitan
Club, New York –
28th May 1988*

Together with Carol

Part II

Maturity

Chapter Five

Skiing

Given my lifelong reluctance to grow up, I suspect that starting the second part of this book under the title 'Maturity' will cause a few smiles. That the children call me 'Peter Pan' is probably even more revealing, but I don't think I am unusual in being reluctant to settle down. My life up to my 30th birthday had been an adventure and I didn't really want this to end. In fact, my new career was something of a new adventure anyway. The main difference being that I was no longer single and so a degree of responsibility reluctantly began to emerge in how I viewed life and in some of the decisions I took.

Before focusing on this new 'mature life', however, there has been one activity that has straddled several phases of my life and which remains my sporting passion to this day, even if it is also responsible for most of my orthopaedic problems. It is my love of skiing. As I have already indicated, skiing became an important means to an end in my social life during my twenties and it is still a wonderful indulgence even now. Heading away from the UK when the skies are grey, the trees bare and the days short, to the crisp air, sunshine and spectacular scenery of the Alps is magic. Couple that with the excitement and competitiveness of skiing and the 'full-on' social life and you have the perfect restorative tonic from whatever of life's pressures you need to recover.

For as long as I can remember, as a child, I had a beautifully crafted and detailed wooden model of a rather grand ski chalet in my bedroom. This Victorian model under a domed glass cover invited me to dream about another world – exotic, glamourous and exciting. It had belonged to my granny, who had been an active skier in Mürren before WWI, and it became my life's wish to buy a place in the Alps where I could live out those dreams. (Incidentally, the modern-day cost of a chalet on that scale would have been prohibitively expensive!) The model, together with Granny's old wooden skis, now adorn our apartment in Klosters, proving that where there is enough determination, dreams can come true!

However, my first skiing holiday was not an auspicious start. I was just about to turn fifteen in 1972 when some great family friends invited me to join their group in Villars. They had invited Sue to ski with them in Saas-Fee a few years earlier and they were very good at involving young family friends and introducing them to winter sports. In fact, I owe them a huge debt of gratitude, even if my first experience ended up in the hospital!

Back then, the equipment was one of the biggest challenges. There were no comfortable and supportive plastic boots (now personally fitted and sometimes even heated). No, these were low, ankle-height leather boots, which dug into the Achilles tendon and seemed to restrict blood flow to the toes, which gradually turned them to ice. Furthermore, skis were selected by measuring to the height of your wrist when your arm was stretched above your head. In my case, my first pair of skis were 205cm long and, unlike the new parabolic-shaped skis of today, which turn almost by themselves, these wooden planks were almost parallel in shape and determined only to go in straight lines. The bindings were very crude Kandahar bindings with a metal spring around the back of the boot clipped down with a big lever in front of the toe binding. Beyond the skis and boots, the clothing was also a bit of a joke. No nice Gore-Tex windproofs, waterproofs or stretchy trousers; it was basically the same as the kit you would use for hiking in the Lake District and so rather inadequate for sub-zero temperatures. To call the kit primitive is putting it mildly, and comfort and safety seemed a long way down the list. However, it all added to the feeling of adventure!

I remember that first trip clearly as it was one of my first overseas holidays and my first flight! We flew out to Basel and then caught the train via Aigle up to Villars. The trip up the mountain on the steep railway track was fantastic, with views out towards Lake Geneva in the west. We were staying at Aiglon College, a 6th form school where, by coincidence, Christopher (Carol's brother) had gone, as had Nick Lamb, our great friend and godfather to Alexandra, and then, much later, William Foyle, our godson. It was typical of a 1970s boarding school – quite basic, rather cold and across a long footbridge from the rest of the town. But being in Switzerland in the winter was such an adventure. The cold air, the fabulous views and lots of exciting new tastes, including *Apfelsaft*, which immediately became my favourite drink.

The first two to three days were spent learning the basics on the nursery slopes, where almost everything seemed totally alien, but I soon discovered that I rather enjoyed balancing on two planks and my gymnastic ability proved invaluable in staying upright and/or getting back to my feet having fallen over.

Turning was always more luck than skill with plenty of crashes and close shaves with other skiers, groups, trees, buildings and almost anything in the way. Stopping seemed to be impossible so I just sat down, which seemed to work and was just as well given that there was a railway track that ran along one side of the nursery slopes. The T-bar lift up the slope was one of the biggest challenges, but clearly essential to master if one had any hope of progressing. By the end of the second day, I had managed to get three quarters of the way up (I was dragged the last thirty yards before I finally let go). Skiing back down was incredible and gave me the taste I now know so well – freedom, excitement and an adrenalin-infused 'high' at the bottom.

Day four, we went up to the top of the mountain with our instructor to a place called Bretaye. The size of the mountain and the range of slopes in every direction is what struck me – the place was enormous. We played 'follow the leader' all over the mountain, trying our best to follow his tracks, even if our steering was still highly unpredictable. It was all going so well until I failed to make a turn and headed straight into some deeper fresh snow on the side of the piste, fell over and broke my ankle. It was the first of many 'blood wagon' journeys off mountains and brought my new sport to a rather abrupt end. However, I had got hooked by the freedom, the exhilaration of adventure and speed, and the whole idea of escaping the grey British winter for the clean, fresh and sunny Alps. This love has stayed with me forever and I can still think of no greater sport for combining so many emotions, healthy exercise, social interaction and excitement.

The trip the following year to Verbier began a bit hesitantly as I retained a healthy nervousness of powder snow. It took a day or two to stop feeling frightened each time I turned through the fall line. But after that, it was all systems go and I am sure my fitness and my natural recklessness gave me a head start. Two further holidays followed in Val d'Isère with the same family friends; it cemented my love of the sport and also introduced me to ski racing, which seemed impossibly exciting. The annual British Championships and Lowlanders' races took place there each January and it was my first time watching the downhill racing on the course at La Daille. I bumped into a couple of school friends who were racing and I thought, *Well, if they can do it, then so can I.*

It was therefore all rather irritating that Royal Marines training interrupted my progression and I had to wait until 1976 before hitting the ski slopes again, this time in Glenshee in Scotland – not quite so glamourous as the Alps, but still fun. It was to be my first time at the Royal Navy ski championships and the basic race training I received there laid the foundations for my racing thereafter. I found that slalom and giant slalom training became addictive with repeated runs to try to improve times. It didn't matter that I was skiing the same slope again and again, it was just about improving technique and speed. Having a dedicated race trainer also provided a very special advantage over the standard resort teachers. The search for precision in corners, using the edges to carve around gates, became a never-ending mission, especially given that ski technology was still pretty basic at the time and it was all too easy to slide and skid rather than carve, thereby losing speed.

One of my abiding memories in Glenshee was watching some brazen queue-barging taking place at the bottom of the T-bar up the infamous (steep and icy) Tiger slope. A young man was being very unsubtle, walking over others in the line and apparently being rather drunk and objectionable. Suddenly, the lift attendant raced out of his small shed armed with an axe, which he then used to chop this poor man's skis to bits to the horror of all those watching. I have never seen such a well-disciplined queue after that, with good manners and politeness the order of the day. It was only later that we discovered this was a traditional trick to impose discipline in the lift line and was all a set-up. Well, it certainly worked!

Those first races in Glenshee shaped my competitive instincts and I realised that with focus and determination I could achieve some success. The early collection of tankards from Glenshee was a wonderful introduction to the competitive sport and my selection for the Royal Navy squad the following season was a huge step forwards. In particular, it gave me the chance to add downhill racing to the slalom and giant slalom disciplines. By comparison to slalom, downhill racing was truly awesome. A clear, fenced-off piste over 2km long, dropping some 800m in height, provides an adrenalin high you can't imagine unless you have done it yourself. My indoctrination was on the fearsome Ischgl downhill in Austria, which began with a precipitous 'wall' followed by an accelerating ride down a series of gulleys before being launched over the final rollers into the finish area. The race was won or lost by the speed captured on the initial 'wall' and how successfully you could maintain this in the bumps and twists thereafter. I was determined not to be found wanting and headed down the wall like a Kamikaze pilot with little real understanding of how I would manage the consequences lower down. I had a series of spectacular crashes, breaking first a binding (it ripped out of the ski), secondly, a ski bent up at right angles and thirdly, a crash into some ice that broke my right thumb. It was another blood wagon trip off the mountain, but the racing bug was firmly implanted.

The racing progressed from there and my downhill form improved to the point where I had a FIS race licence and international points, which allowed me to race in different events around the Alps. The limitation was that I was still a serving Royal Marines officer, but I must admit to having had considerable freedom to race in the British Championships

(7th was my best downhill result), various Lowlanders, Citadin and even one Europa Cup race. But the major races from my perspective were the navy, army and inter-services events – after all, they were sponsoring me! The five-year period between 1979 and 1984 probably marked my peak years, part of which was over my exchange time with the army. During that time, I won the army downhill both years and was inter-services runner-up twice. That I never won the inter-services downhill is very disappointing, but I have a picture of me, at the moment my binding has released on landing, in the one race I could have won, when I was over a second ahead at the mid-point and just had that last big jump to negotiate. How cruel racing can sometimes be!

While downhill was my favourite, I also had to master the two slalom disciplines, which involved tighter turns and, in the case of slalom, navigating through a maze of gates that had to be carefully learned and memorised to avoid missing one in the race. I did win a few slalom races, but generally found them a bit 'frantic', battering poles out of the way as I raced down.

On one occasion before the advent of the modern elastic-mounted poles, which fold flat when you hit them, I was racing with old-fashioned wooden poles. These not only hurt when you hit them, but meant that you had to ski a more rounded course. As I progressed down the course, I reached the final verticale and was beginning to let my speed go as I could see the finish, when, unfortunately, the tip of my ski hit a pole head on, causing it to fly out and cartwheel down the course ahead of me, before embedding itself in the snow upside down with the point sticking up – rather like an Agincourt stake. The impact with the pole had knocked me off balance and I tumbled down through the course, before coming to rest to find the pole sticking up between my legs, through my ski trousers. Later that day, when I got home, I found that the pole had gone through my ski trousers, long johns and underpants, but miraculously missed everything else – it must have been very cold that day! The whole chapter on children, which follows, might never have happened!

Giant slalom was, in fact, the most useful discipline to master as it didn't require the fenced-off and regulated piste of a downhill, but was still fast and technical. I still race GS even now and enjoy the precision and challenge of competition, even if family and others are now faster! In fact, GS was my most reliable event statistically; I was always in the points and had a dependable ability to complete the courses, having only 'blown out' once in over thirty years of racing.

In that context, injuries probably deserve a short paragraph as I seem to have picked up quite a few over the last fifty years of skiing and far more than in any other activity. Perhaps this is because I was always determined to let myself go and not hold back. Racing (certainly downhill racing) is typically about that fine balance between control and total abandon, with plenty of moments when, to be honest, there is no semblance of control. But as a young, athletic racer, millisecond adjustments to position, weight, balance, etc. mark the difference between success and failure, and life is on the edge. What I have unfortunately experienced over the last fifteen to twenty years, however, is that the same instinctive reactions to recover from an impending catastrophe are seriously handicapped by ageing muscles and reluctant joints. So while the mind may be willing, the body is patently and sometimes pathetically weak. This explains why my injuries straddle two phases of my skiing life, the first being my competitive years when falls resulted from overambition and pure recklessness; and my later years when accidents happened because my self-preservation instincts were let down by an ageing body!

One of my most unpleasant accidents occurred while skiing gently with Carol down to join the rest of the family for lunch. I foolishly decided to take a detour over three big rolling bumps, which were part of the Davos 'Fun Park'. I ended up carrying far too much speed through the first bump, so ended up with huge backward rotation as I landed and was immediately launched up by the second bump. Landing upside down on the top of the third bump resulted in a dislocated elbow as I tried to break my fall, a broken sacrum joint in my pelvis and a broken vertebra. Not a happy end to what was supposed to be a gentle run down to lunch and so much for the fun park!

For the record, my breakages to date are as follows:

Anatomy	Cause
Left ankle (lower fibula)	Skiing
Right ankle (a little bone in the joint)	Parachuting
Nose	Rugby
Right middle finger	Rugby
Right thumb	Skiing
Left wrist	Skiing
L4 and L5 vertebrae (compression)	Skiing / Parachuting
Right heel	Falling off haystack
Ribs x 2	Skiing
	(falling over Alexandra, to be precise)
Right shoulder	Motorcycle accident
Dislocated left elbow	Skiing
T12 vertebra	Skiing
Pelvis (five fractures in two accidents)	Skiing
Left ACL in knee	Skiing

This is not a list in which I take any pride and I know masks the stress and worry of Carol (and our GP) who dread the next long-distance phone call from an A&E ward!

There are a handful of memories that stand out for me from

all my years skiing and I will share a few now. At the top of the list has to be the sense of pure exhilaration as you finish a downhill race and flash through the finish gate in front of a huge crowd of spectators. The mixture of adrenalin, euphoria, relief and excitement is impossible to beat. The heart is still pumping flat out, but all you want to see is your time flash up on the board and check if you have won or (more importantly) beaten your arch-rival. I have been lucky enough to win several downhills and it is the most overwhelming sense of relief and fulfilment, tempered by all those moments where you made a mistake but recovered, or made a mistake and lost the race. Once a racer, always a racer is my experience, and I am determined never to lose my competitive instinct.

I have also had a few close shaves, one of which could have been the end of me. I was racing with the army in Ischgl, Austria in 1980 where there had been a huge snowfall. After our GS race, I had a couple of hours to kill before it was dark and decided to chase off and find the powder. I was with my girlfriend, Debbie, at the time and after nearly two hours, I wanted to do one last run down an untouched valley above the town. Debbie sensibly decided to ski down the piste and we agreed to meet in the bar at the bottom. The snow in the valley must have been six-feet deep, light and fluffy, and I was soon at the bottom after a wonderful, liberating and exhausting run. I then realised that I was in a hanging valley with a waterfall at the end and there was no way to ski back down to the town. So I had no choice but to try and climb back up more than 300m vertical height and at least one km in distance back to the piste – easier said than done in six feet of fresh powder. I was still wearing my 210cm GS skis, which proved hopelessly impractical in the deep snow. After thirty minutes trying to scale the valley side, I decided to try walking up the flatter and more open valley floor. The first few metres were fine, but I then suddenly fell through the snow, landing in the waist-deep, freezing water of the stream flowing underneath. As I fell through, my skis, which I had been carrying on my shoulder – bridged the hole and I was just hanging onto them as the pile of snow under my feet was rapidly washed away. Using all my strength I managed to pull myself back up onto the surface, but I was now freezing cold from the waist down and sweating from the waist up. It was also getting dark and it was abundantly clear that no one knew I was there. It took me about two and a half hours to get back up to the piste after a totally exhausting marathon in the deep snow. All the while, I was concerned that Debbie must be worried sick about me. It was pitch-dark and I suspected that she must have sent search teams out to scour the slopes and valleys. I was rather less than impressed to find her lying in the bath when I got back to our room, without any apparent idea that I had been fighting for my life! It was just as well I was so fit, as it could easily have ended very badly.

Happier memories include completing the Haute Route from Chamonix with a group of ex-army skiers. Sadly, we had to end our attempt at Arolla as the final section into Zermatt was dangerous with the weather closing in. But the freedom of being literally up in the top of the mountains and staying in little mountain refuges was fabulous, and created a very tight-knit sense of identity and purpose as we sought to beat other groups slogging their way up hills on their touring skis and skins. At times, we all roped up with crampons to climb up steep gulleys, only to enjoy the exhilaration of a run down the other side, creating our own tracks on virgin snow. We quickly adopted a very disparaging attitude towards normal tourist skiers who took the lifts (like any normal person would), but had enormous fun showing off our telemark turns as we raced each other down the slopes around Verbier and the other resorts en route. I only wished that I had done the tour when I had been serving in the RM rather than five years after I left, by which time I was considerably less fit.

The same might be said for the week of heli-skiing in Canada with some German friends. Once again, the sense of liberation you experience when landing on the peak of a mountain miles from anywhere, with fresh snow in every direction, is spectacular. We were all good skiers and, with a dedicated helicopter, it meant that we were only limited by our fitness and skiing ability. We quickly realised that we could challenge the world record for the vertical meterage skied in one day and in one week. It meant that we would race down the mountains, powder snow 'smoking' in our wake as we snaked through trees, around the crevasses of the glaciers and over huge jumps; the latter normally ending in a massive pile up or with someone buried in a tree hole. At the end of the day, all we could do was soak in a hot bath, get a deep tissue massage for our weary limbs, eat a huge meal and then hit the sack. The achievement, however, was a new world record, which we registered with the *Guinness World Records* of 24,000 vertical metres skied in one day and over 110,000 in six days. It was pretty exceptional for a group of seven tourists!

I could easily write an entire book just on my skiing stories and the wonderful (and sometimes less wonderful) memories. But the fact is that skiing holidays are the perfect combination of adventure, excitement, healthy exercise, social interaction and over-eating (and occasional danger). It brings family and friends together and provides an ideal environment for dissipating work stress and other worries. It really is the best sport in the world and I am truly thrilled that all the family love it as much as I do.

My first ski trip in Villars, Switzerland – 1972

Broken ankle – day three

*The Royal Navy Ski
Championships –
1976*

*British
Championships
at Val d'Isère –
1977*

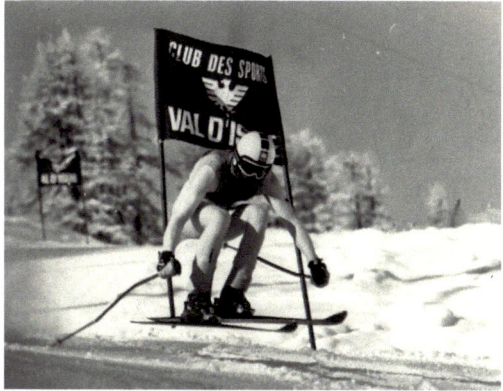

*Early success:
7th in British
Championships –
1978*

*Inter-services in
Valloire – 1982
(NB: damaged
negative, not
breaking the sound
barrier!)*

*Europa Cup
vorlaufer in
Valloire – 1982*

Royal Navy team – c1981

Some of the silverware from my time skiing with the Army

Royal Marines champion – 1985

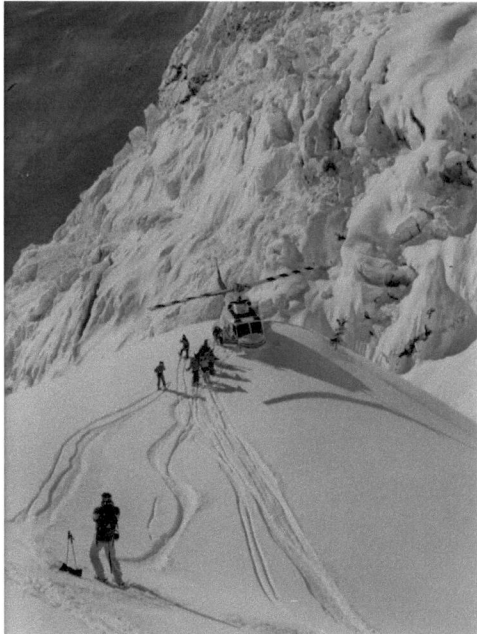

On our way to a heli-skiing world record in Canada – 1996

Slalom action – c1982

GS action – 2023

Chapter Six

Family

There is a blissful period following marriage when life is totally focused around the one person you most want to be with, indulging in all the things you most want to do. It is probably the last truly selfish phase when there is nothing to worry about beyond work and what to do the next weekend. True, the first six months after our wedding were spent launching me into a new career with the attendant worries of learning a whole new financial language and skill set, but, looking back, it was a wonderfully enjoyable period for both of us. Carol and I took every opportunity to go on impromptu visits and long weekend trips, and the spontaneity as well as financial freedom we enjoyed was truly liberating. Our last breath of independence was a holiday to Indonesia where we visited the ancient Buddhist temples, volcanoes and famous Komodo dragons. Back in 1989, Indonesia was still remarkably primitive, but incredibly rich in culture and history. It was also possibly the most populated place I had ever been to with people popping up everywhere. On one inviting, romantic and – we thought – deserted beach, we decided to take a skinny dip, only to turn around after fifteen minutes or so in the water to see about twenty people gathered around our bags and clothes, waiting to sell us bananas and bracelets etc. I was elected to walk back stark naked to disperse them!

Little did we know how much the arrival of Victoria in February 1990 would change our lives. This somehow sounds resentful, but is, in fact, quite the opposite. It is hard to imagine how the total dependence of a young baby can so change one's priorities, outlook and capacity to love. In true Victoria fashion, she arrived late – in fact, it seemed that she had no intention of vacating her warm and cosy home. Eventually, though, she was reluctantly delivered after a marathon 24-hour induced labour. Sitting at the 'business end' to watch, it was both horrific and miraculous in equal measure, but an incredible and unmissable experience. Mothers descended from both Salisbury and New York to dispense wisdom and knowledge, most of which went straight over my head as I quickly realised this was not really my show at all and all I needed to do was to try and keep an even keel on broader family responsibilities.

But it did abruptly mark the transition from self-centred and spontaneous living to planning ahead, maternity nurses, nannies and 'stuff'… lots and lots of stuff. It is hard to believe how much stuff is needed and has to be carried around for something so small. Away went the fun two-door BMW in favour of a sensible five-door SAAB. The garage at Flood Street - our new marital home, became a parking place for a huge antique London Baby Carriage pram (like a Silver Cross pram, but bigger) and push chairs, child seats, play pens, cots, strollers, toys, etc. It was just as well that we had a large house, as each room in turn filled up. And with all the clobber came a whole new routine, which took over the house from dawn to dusk and during the night, too, with midnight feeds, etc. Since I couldn't dispense milk myself, I was saved the midnight shift and counted myself lucky to escape to work in the morning. It was a bit bewildering, to be honest, but our wonderful maternity nurse gradually established a routine and a semblance of normality returned to the house. However, privacy was one of the early casualties and we learned that for the foreseeable future we would be sharing the house with all and sundry.

The journey of parenthood is unique. It also marks the first realisation that life's cycle continues, relentlessly almost, and it is both irritating and amusing to hear oneself saying the same things that made one cringe as a child. The values embedded in us as children are among the most enduring and certainly shape our early years, even if they gradually adapt to new partners, input and/or circumstances. Parenthood carries with it a huge responsibility for providing moral guidance and direction, but equally it provides a special opportunity to pass on standards and beliefs that are meaningful to oneself. It is somewhat inevitable that one's initial instincts revert to those we all remember as children and so the cycle continues. Although our childhoods and backgrounds were very different, Carol and I shared many similar values and instincts about things, and where we didn't, her view normally prevailed anyway! But we had very few arguments about how to bring the children up and we simply doted on Victoria, then Alexandra and, in due course, Robert, as they began to develop their own characters and styles, sharing those truly special and unforgettable memories of first steps, first words and the never-ending list of 'firsts' that is the joy of parenthood. It also proved to be a wonderful opportunity for me to relive my own childhood, semi-vicariously, through them and the fact that Victoria and Alexandra weren't boys made no difference at all as far as I was concerned.

Just before Victoria was born, we had been fortunate enough to buy Bottom Farm, a lovely Queen Anne farmhouse nestling in the Chiltern Hills, a few miles from Henley. This became our weekly escape from London, offering all the varieties of the countryside and the chance to create some wonderful memories for the children. Sandpits in the old chicken run; a tree house in the yew tree (complete with a basket on a rope to bring up dolls, tea and biscuits, etc.); all sorts of places to hide and explore; and long Sunday walks and cycle rides. It was paradise and remains so in all our hearts, being a unique and almost protected world where we could, and still can, relax and be ourselves. It was wonderfully introverted family time where we could make our own adventures together, learning how to amuse ourselves rather than needing to be entertained. In fact, Bottom Farm became the focus for nearly all our family adventures, and these gradually evolved as we refurbished first the house, then the garden and lastly the barns – all nine of them! We all found ways to add our own personal touches and it is fair to say that Bottom Farm largely defines us as a family, being so full of happy memories, sitting as it does in an unspoilt valley, surrounded by a special tranquillity and the sound of birdsong. It was very special to watch first Victoria and then Alexandra, eighteen months later, hold their wedding receptions down by the lake, surrounded by the sights and smells of their childhood home and all the memories that went with that.

But this is to jump ahead slightly in the story. Victoria and Alexandra, although quite different, became inseparable, playing with their dolls, dressing up together and generally getting into mischief. Victoria, being the older, assumed the role of boss (something she still tries to retain), but Alexandra was a willing accomplice and we would often find piles of empty sweet wrappers in strange places, where they had held an impromptu feast with their dolls. Bottom Farm provided a wonderful backdrop for their adventures and imagination, and there are probably few corners that they didn't explore together. Alexandra developed child asthma quite early on, which required twice daily sessions on the nebuliser and meant that she was quite vulnerable in her early years. We discovered much later that Victoria had also kept her effectively comatose on liberal extra spoonfuls of Calpol at night, which probably explained why Alexandra was so quiet much of the time in those early years. But the pre-school years were full of incredibly happy memories and I think that only now can the girls recognise and value the role that Carol played as a full-time mother at home to look after them, even though we had nannies to attend to much of the routine work.

One of the challenges of parenthood is to allocate enough time to enjoy one's children, rather than just being the ship that (literally) passes in the night. It is always sad to meet people who realise, in hindsight, that without having made a conscious decision, they simply missed out on spending very much time with their children, focusing instead on their work and all the other myriad of distractions that exist. And, wow, how fast time can fly by! I was determined to allocate enough time to the family and created strict barriers between my work and home life, rather as I had done in the military. I was also determined not to take work home and I would prefer to work another hour in the office and finish a task, rather than get on the slippery slope and bring office priorities home. How much easier that was in the 1980s and 1990s before the internet and mobile phones! In the 1990s, email and mobile working was still in its infancy and I was incredibly lucky to enjoy working hours that were relatively civilised. It meant that I would be able to have breakfast every day with the girls and see them for a good thirty minutes before their day started. Although this sounds ridiculously short, it was a regular and important time for all of us. Bath time was always harder to enjoy as I ran the risk of rushing home and firing the girls up just as Carol was trying to get them to relax, ready for bed. Accordingly, outside weekends, I normally missed bath time. However, 'gardening leave' – the period between jobs – was always a great chance to spend time during the day and I used to love walking the girls to or from school, playing games and telling stories. I still have vivid memories of Alexandra running ahead to hide in order to jump out and frighten me. Most of the time this worked out fine, but a few hapless strangers occasionally got the fright of their lives when they walked into an ambush.

Storytelling became part of these early memories, just as they had for me. My father used to tell us his 'Stephen and Henry stories', which he made up as he went along to amuse and distract us. I realised that this was a wonderful way to engage with the girls and, later on, with Robert, and I developed quite a repertoire of stories that often started with the girls giving me the first sentence from which I had to develop a plot. For the sake of gender diversity and because of wanting the girls to feel involved, I added two new names to this unlikely gang of characters, Harriet and Imogen. Thereafter, my stories were always about this rather odd group of four, but what fun it was. The best stories would often go on for days, drawn out at bedtime to give them something to dream about, and stories such as 'the chocolate factory', 'the avalanche' and 'the jungle' became almost legendary. I recall that Robert was always very specific about his stories, which nearly always had to include pirates and/or soldiers and a variety of galleons and treasure, and he became agitated if the plot didn't go along the lines he wanted! This probably marked the end of that phase of storytelling, but looking back it was enormous fun, mixing up all sorts of real life and fictional stories, films, books, etc. and sensing the engagement of the children as they hung on every word. It was hugely rewarding.

Growing up in a houseful of girls hadn't really troubled me up to this point. True, I was surrounded by dolls, frou-frou skirts and prams, but I built them tree houses, adventure areas and we spent most weekends in the garden. Remember that this was my second childhood, too! But the arrival of Robert, six and a half years after Alexandra, opened up a whole new dimension I hadn't realised I was missing. I quickly discovered how special it was to have a son on whom to focus specific 'boy stuff' and in whom to try and sow some seeds of manly interest. Robert was wonderfully unconstrained and possessed a most extraordinary imagination. He would entertain us as a pirate, shop keeper, restaurateur or singer, and had (and still has) a great gift as a mimic. Suddenly, the house seemed to explode with activity and we quickly realised that going from two to three was a quantum change. The girls seemed to welcome this interloper readily, despite the turmoil, and so life quickly moved on. It was only sad that the girls were just too far ahead in age and development to want to play with him and involve him in their games. It meant that Robert had to rely largely on his own imagination as he had no immediate sibling to play with, but we weren't about to have another child just to keep him company!

With Robert still tackling Captain Hook or entertaining an imaginary guest in his restaurant, life was beginning to become more important for the girls with the academic conveyor belt just beginning to unfold. The challenge of finding the right school is possibly one of the most stressful responsibilities for a parent. Quite apart from the costs of private education and the inevitable financial sacrifice this entails, there is a whole academic, social, sporting and cultural agenda. The normal default is to consider one's own school but since Carol was educated in the US, this wasn't an option. We decided on Downe House, an all-girls boarding school in Berkshire in the aptly named Cold Ash. It was strange to leave Victoria there aged eleven with a bunch of other girls all looking rather vulnerable and alone. It brought back memories of my teary-eyed first day at Marlborough House all those years before and I realised that my own parents must have found it just as traumatic leaving me back then as I did leaving Victoria thirty years later. However, Carol seemed to be made of sterner stuff and gave me no time for self-pity! For her part, Victoria loved her new-found independence from home and seemed to get into all sorts of scrapes and adventures, possibly some of my stories fuelling her imagination. But I was thrilled that she could indulge in some of the adventures that are so important to growing up, part of which is learning how to adapt behaviour when you get caught! We also discovered that she could be somewhat economical with the truth when it suited her and sometimes she managed to dig herself even deeper holes trying to wriggle out of something.

Alexandra blossomed on her own at her London prep school once Victoria had left, although her year group contained a somewhat eclectic group of girls. But away from Victoria's shadow, her confidence grew enormously, and she developed a wonderful sense of humour and a down-to-earth candour that she retains to this day. Independence from Victoria was good for her and prepared her well for the early terms at Downe House that followed. She quickly established a reputation for herself on the sports field and in athletics, where she and Victoria often raced head to head in events. I would not dare say who was the better athlete, but Alexandra went on to be captain of athletics and both held various school records.

School life suited them in different ways and they both managed to balance their different academic, sporting and social agendas. One of my favourite school memories is of visiting them during their terms in France in a little town called Veyrines-de-Domme in the Dordogne. This term was supposed to give the girls a head start in French (questionable, in my view) and to get away from the normal school routines. It also allowed parents to visit for a long weekend each side of the half term and Carol and I split this so we each had time alone with the girls. This provided some important 'one-on-one' time and

I recall some very funny and loving moments. It was a special time with them and one of the last moments before the pressure of exams took over. I have very fond memories of each weekend, particularly the second one when I had to race back to the UK by car for a job interview with J.P. Morgan, the day after an air traffic controllers' strike in France prevented a more leisurely return home.

Robert, meanwhile, was also growing up. Having reluctantly discarded his pirate phase, he still appeared to prefer life in an imaginary world of fantasy and was slow to knuckle down to school life and classwork. Interestingly, he seemed much more comfortable with adults than with contemporaries and perhaps this was a result of him having much older siblings. However, he was an independent spirit who didn't need or look for approval, and these traits have stood him well through the rough and tumble of school life, even if he wasn't always 'one of the gang'. Needless to say, he loved the school plays and any opportunity to dress up (he was normally cast as the girl), and he learned to play to the audience in lots of different ways.

We sent Robert to Horris Hill prep school when he was eight and a half, having carefully chosen the school with the right mix of teachers, culture and environment in which he could grow up gently and begin to learn the responsibilities of life. He was keen to go away to boarding school, having watched the girls go off to Downe House, so it seemed logical to let him get used to boarding even though he was still very young. It was therefore very unfortunate that the headmaster changed the very term Robert arrived and, with him, much of the character and uniqueness of the school. The incoming head didn't warm to Robert and we were disappointed by his management of the school. Oh, what joys parenthood can so often throw at you! However, as an old-fashioned school, it did provide lots of great memories for Robert, from bonfire and fireworks nights to school plays and sports. He was in the thick of things most of the time and, towards the end of his time there, he learned the value of having two very pretty elder sisters to come and visit him.

Cheltenham College was always going to be a big step up after Horris Hill and early days didn't bode well after Robert was on the receiving end of bullying behaviour, which seemed to drive him into his shell. It was a bit of a low point for him and we spent many anxious nights wondering if we should move him and, if so, where to. But gradually through a combination of action from the housemaster and the slow fact of growing up, Robert developed an inner robustness and a determination to succeed, which has been his hallmark ever since.

I will not develop the journeys of each child further as it is best described as 'work in progress'. However, watching them grow up, meet the trials of school and national exams and then transition on into university, is both stressful yet also hugely rewarding. This journey through the ranks of school prefects, house captains, lead actors, county athletics selection, etc. provides multiple opportunities to revel in their successes and I have been immensely proud of all three. They are each very different and yet have emerged as strong individuals in their own rights with a sense of purpose and direction, which is enviable. The girls are now both well established in their careers and Robert is on the cusp of his. What more could a parent ask for?

However, I realise that as I write this, the one truism about being a parent is that you never stop worrying about your children. It is impossible not to agonise about something, whether it is of your making or theirs. We tried to make the right calls, but inevitably we made many mistakes. I think it is much harder being a parent during a child's adolescence and some of the trickiest moments can arise from too much parental direction, yielding completely the opposite result. By the time a child is an adolescent, their character is quite well established and what they need more is encouragement and gentle guidance to help develop their own judgement. Our role should be to equip them to make the best choices on their own.

I have had, and continue to have, the most wonderful time as a father and share countless happy memories with Victoria, Alexandra and Robert both individually and collectively. I love each unquestioningly, yet also differently. Not more or less or better or worse, but simply differently, reflecting the evolution of each relationship. In this respect, I feel lucky to have spent time with each when we could get to know each other more as individuals rather than simply as parent and child. In fact, some of my happiest and funniest memories are with them when we were supposedly grown-up! May that always be the case.

Interestingly, looking back over this chapter, I realise it has been the hardest to write so far and there is an element of philosophical reflection that underlies the narrative. Perhaps it is a desire to be approved as a parent or to justify certain actions! But there is no doubt that being a parent has proven to be the most fulfilling part of my life even if I got plenty of things wrong or was unable to provide everything I would have liked to give. The conflict between wanting everything for your children and yet also wanting them to be ambitious and confident enough to go out there and achieve it themselves is part of the tightrope of parenthood. I feel sad for those couples who cannot or choose not to have children as they can't experience the complexity and extra dimension that raising children brings to a marriage. To my mind, it has given me a sense of purpose for my marriage with Carol beyond that of just simple enjoyment or selfish pleasures. I do so hope that Victoria, Alexandra and Robert will share this same feeling as their lives unfold.

Bottom Farm House

The garden at Bottom Farm

Robert in early classic pose

Enforced Christmas card photo – 2006

Robert, Victoria and Alexandra at our 25th anniversary party,
'Out of Africa' – 2013

'Out of Africa' party – 2013

Royal Ascot – c2015

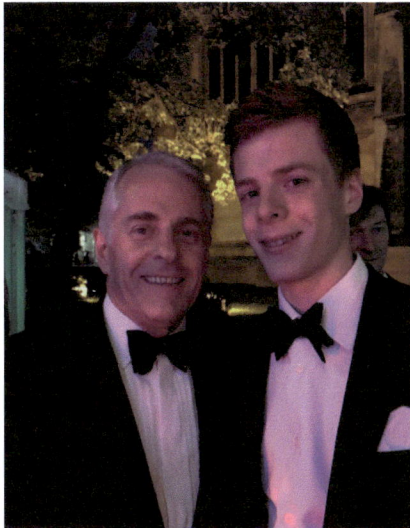

*Robert at the Cheltenham leavers' ball
– 2016*

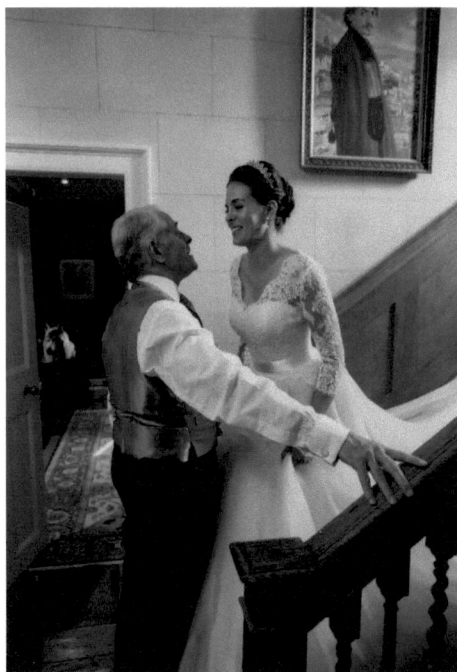

*Victoria's wedding day
– 9th September 2017*

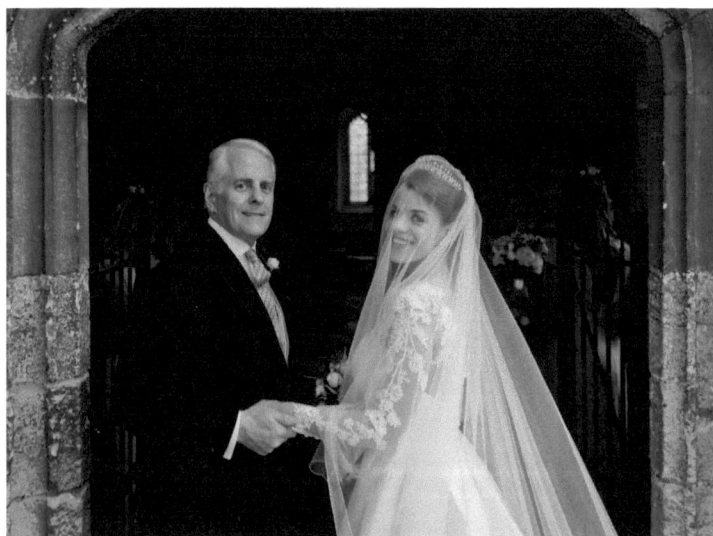

Alexandra's wedding day – 15th June 2019

Chapter Seven

The City

Starting a new career after twelve years in the Royal Marines was both exciting and daunting in equal measure. The same worries I had felt listening to careers lectures at school returned to haunt me, wondering what on earth I might actually be any good at or, better still, might enjoy. At the time, the country was getting used to Thatcherite capitalism and the City was starting to boom with 'Big Bang' – the deregulation of the stock market in 1986. With that came a wave of mergers and takeovers of many of the previously somewhat introverted City institutions, and horizons expanded exponentially as exchange controls and other barriers disappeared. Suddenly, we were surrounded with rather obnoxious yuppies, shouting into their mobile phones (the size of a house brick), and greed became the mantra. Gordon Gekko had his UK equivalent and London saw its own 'Bonfire of the Vanities'.

A number of former RMs had preceded me into the City by

then and they encouraged me to look into a career as a broker. One immediate problem, however, was my total ignorance of finance or even basic commercial know-how. The Royal Marines had kindly sent me off on a resettlement course at Hatfield Polytechnic (now the University of Hertfordshire) in the autumn of 1987, where I took the first part of a Diploma of Management Science. It was essentially a poor man's MBA, but introduced me to the commercial world and ended with exam modules in accounting, law, marketing, etc., which provided me with a basic business understanding. It also taught me that I didn't want to be an accountant or a lawyer, but that advertising, marketing and sales sounded quite interesting. So, on return from honeymoon in the summer of 1988, I began the process of job applications and interviews and networking as hard as I could with old school friends and the military community. Back then, it didn't actually help very much that I had been in the services as a military career was rather unfashionable with little going on apart from Northern Ireland and the 'one-off' Falklands. 'Anyone who was anyone' was thrusting their way forwards in the City already.

Mercury Asset Management

Getting used to rejection became the norm. However, rather like buses, two opportunities came along at the same time and suddenly I had traction. The first was with a small headhunting business, which intrigued me because it appealed to my desire to get close to people and find out what makes them tick, then try and help them. However, as I was finalising details to join this firm, a referral from an old school friend put me in touch with David Rosier, an ex-army man who was running the newly amalgamated private client investment team of Mercury Asset Management, the separately listed arm of S.G. Warburg. The

S.G. Warburg Group ('SGW') was, at the time, one of the top blue-chip UK banking institutions and an opportunity to join them was too hard to pass up. Despite having got rather a long way down the road with the small headhunter, I jettisoned his offer and joined the SGW graduate training scheme (as a rather mature non-graduate) in mid-October 1988. My role being to understudy the marketing director of the private client group. I learned later that my salary composed the residual, non-spent part of the 1988 advertising budget that they had cancelled! A grand total of £18,000, which was even less than I had been earning as a Royal Marines officer!

It proved to be the best possible start to my new career and provided a platform of professionalism and training that would serve me well for the next thirty years. SGW set and expected high standards and the bank appeared to run with almost military precision. Siegmund Warburg himself had imposed a very strict code of conduct and business disciplines, and Mercury Asset Management ('MAM') followed these assiduously. This included handwriting analysis for all new employees (it is amazing I passed, given the illegibility of my handwriting!); meeting notes written on yellow, white, pink or blue paper according to whether they were advisory, management, required a decision, were HR-related, etc.; and a host of other written and unwritten codes and protocols that had to be learned. Integrity and duty were engrained in everyone and these were values I readily understood and recognised, making my transition all the easier. I quickly adapted to the new financial vernacular, the structured life and long hours, and became immensely grateful to have found myself part of an organisation with the same work ethics and standards I had grown used to in the Royal Marines.

My immediate role was to help the business development director of the private client group acquire new clients and spread the word about how good we were. Our main competitors then were the likes of Kleinwort Benson, Lazard, Schroders, Cazenove, etc. as the Swiss and American firms were only really beginning to raise their UK profiles. New clients appeared to be sourced, almost equally, from one of three main areas: by referral from the investment bank or corporate broking department; by referral from an existing client; and/or by referral from an external adviser, such as a lawyer, accountant or trustee. It was believed that the main focus of our marketing should be on developing relationships with the leading advisers, or intermediaries as we called them, since this would leverage our reach beyond what the group itself and our own client base could deliver. Looking back, we could, in fact, have done so much more by working harder on the other two areas of referral, but rather assumed that everyone would be good at cross-marketing and left them to it. This, of course, was well before the 'hard sell' and 'cold call' tactics that now almost exclusively dominate client acquisition in the private banking arena.

Computerisation was beginning to hit all areas of life in the 1980s, not least the City, and one of my earliest roles was to input the intermediary database and then the prospective client database onto a Lotus 1-2-3 programme in order to be able to track and manage our contacts. It was early days for computers with plenty of crashes, wiping out a day's worth of entry, and patience could wear thin. Gradually, though, the flexibility of being able to manipulate information on screen and then produce a report or chart became evident. I remember printing off a 3D asset allocation chart on Harvard Graphics (a software graphics programme) for a client meeting with strange pride. It was a first at MAM and much remarked on by our clients at the time.

During those early days, I would attend as many meetings as I could with the fund managers and gradually learn the story of what we did, how and why. I also watched in admiration at how some managers managed to wriggle out of difficult questions, make mediocre performance sound acceptable and win over new clients on barely more than flimsy promises! We were selling security, peace of mind and institutionalised continuity – and it proved very attractive.

What I was also gaining, although was perhaps less aware of at the time, was an introduction to a whole generation of top-quality private client advisers from across London and the primary regional centres. The young partners I was meeting at law firms or offshore trustee companies became real friends and I have stayed close to many as we have gradually edged our way up our respective corporate ladders. I now know many of the leading partners across the private client community and this has been extraordinarily worthwhile, both personally and professionally. It was highly fortuitous that MAM was one of the top institutions in the late '80s and early '90s and, as a result, intermediaries wanted to stay close to us and, consequently, we had a privileged access to their top clients. In the process, I realised that by understanding the tax and legal issues being handled by the advisers, I could relate more readily to them and ensure that I could advise teams internally on any tax restrictions or complications that might affect their accounts. This proved very rewarding both as a way of generating credibility with the advisers, but also to my own understanding of client needs and priorities. I became a member of the Society of Trust and Estate Practitioners during my time at MAM, reflecting the extent of my interest in this part of the overall client proposition.

The tight-knit nature of the business created a strong team environment and we had an active social life beyond the office. We also hosted a lot of corporate hospitality events with golf, opera, concerts, art galleries, etc. providing a regular opportunity to mingle with clients or intermediaries outside work. In the peaceful pre-email and BlackBerry world, this provided a great way to mingle work and pleasure and was well proven as a means of getting to know clients and cement relationships or win trust. Shortly after my arrival, I was asked to help host one of the group's key events of the year: the Open Golf Championship at St Andrews. This was mainly reserved for the top pension fund clients of the institutional side of the group and was a high-profile and expensive event involving everyone from the most senior management team. I was seen as a useful extra pair of hands and so joined the group at Balcarres, a large Scottish castle about fifteen minutes away from St Andrews. MAM had rented the house to provide a suitably memorable occasion for guests, who would stay a couple of nights in the house and attend the golf. It was to prove the scene of one of my more embarrassing experiences and a cause for endless ribbing at the time!

I was despatched to Edinburgh Airport to meet the London flight on which six of our guests were travelling, including the wife of the deputy chairman and the husband of Carol Galley – the head of our pensions business (aka the 'Ice Maiden'). Also in the group were a Jersey senator and some other 'big wigs'. I arrived well on time and hired a second car, which I would ask one of the group to drive so we could fit everyone in and travel in convoy to Fife (yes, I know, we should have organised a bus!). The first challenge came when none of the arriving guests wanted to drive as they had been drinking on the flight up. I finally managed to persuade one and we all loaded up, ready to set off. I then discovered that I had locked the keys for my car in my briefcase in the boot and the lid required a key to open it rather than just being a button. After trying (and failing) to think of an alternative, I eventually asked my passengers to get out of the car and dismantled the back seat to burrow into the boot to salvage my briefcase. Having retrieved the keys, I got back into the car to drive off and only then noticed a button down by my seat indicating a boot release catch! Still, we were now only fifteen minutes late, so we had plenty of time, although the Edinburgh rush-hour traffic was to be our next hazard.

Driving in convoy is always tricky, but I kept a close eye on the car behind as we weaved our way through the traffic to the Forth Road Bridge. It was not an easy journey, but I thought we were making good time as I stopped at the toll booth to wait for the other car. When they arrived, I got an earful of abuse for driving too fast, for trying my best to lose them in the traffic and, last but not least, for being inconsiderate to the guest who was driving – who, unknown to me until then, had a severe heart condition. This dressing-down was delivered forcefully by the deputy chairman's wife (who I had never met before) and, as we set off over the bridge, I was convinced that my short career at MAM was probably over. I was also terrified of driving too fast, despite the time pressure to get to the castle for dinner. In fact, I was so intent on not going too fast that I managed to take a wrong turn on the outskirts of Inverkeithing and we ended up in a cul-de-sac in a dreary council estate. Ignominy is not a strong enough word to convey the depth of humiliation I felt as I saw the looks of the passengers in the accompanying car as we all did a U-turn. I thought that if I hadn't scuppered my career at the bridge, I certainly had by now! The final forty-five minutes home were spent with my passengers, the senator and his wife from Jersey, being incredibly sweet to me, saying it could have happened to anyone and not to worry! It was certainly a low point, but, in fact, over the course of the next few days, everyone came to see the funny side and just teased me. It was probably an unusual but effective way of getting to know senior management.

Those early years at MAM were a constant learning process when it came to the business of winning clients and delivering value, but I was also becoming aware of internal management issues and strategic direction and began to see an opportunity to progress my own career within the company. Perhaps the military routine of two-year assignments and then moving on was the impetus to continually seek progress up the 'greasy pole' of management, but, whatever it was, I sensed a chance to contribute to the business as well as work on client acquisition. The head of the marketing department had left about eighteen months after I arrived and I had taken over his responsibilities. In this respect, I had earned the support of the head of the department and was fortunate to be promoted progressively up to 'director' during the early years. However, the business had grown considerably and there was a need for a more dedicated international client development effort. Accordingly, an experienced international marketing head arrived, giving me more time to focus on UK activity and, curiously, the development of our US interests.

Given Carol's US status and the regular dialogue we had with the managers of her affairs in New York, I was familiar with the very US-centric mindset of most US-based managers. The typical allocation was very skewed to the US markets with minimal international investment and currency diversification. True, the US market was the dominant global market, and still is, but I thought that there must be plenty of internationally minded people, like us, who wanted to adopt a more global investment approach. London was rapidly developing its role as a global financial centre and I felt certain that the international status of a London-based manager would carry kudos and strong attraction for many US-based clients. I also wanted to explore the management of investment portfolios for US persons living outside the US. Presenting an understanding, and potentially a solution, to US investment and tax complexities would, I believed, be a differentiator in London, especially among the intermediary community of tax specialists.

Initially, though, my focus was to develop an international product offering in the US itself, presenting London and

Warburg as a viable platform for internationally minded US residents (NB: although branded 'Mercury Asset Management' for all UK business, MAM adopted the Warburg name for international clients, which proved valuable in the US). To achieve credibility and momentum in the US, we decided to work with a US-based partner to help distribute our profile and products and, critically, provide the direct client contact. The MAM board agreed to let me explore this further and, together with a senior MD from the main board, we planned our first visit in early 1992. I had by then lined up Smith Barney, one of the major 'white-shoe' brokers in the US, as a potential partner, following an introduction from one of Carol's fund managers.

The trip was memorable on multiple levels, but flying out on Concorde was one! British Airways were offering a very tempting upgrade at the time for business class ticket holders. It was too big an opportunity to miss and a very special feeling to enjoy the enhanced first class treatment and prestige of going to the Concorde check-in and arrive in New York only three hours later. I took mementoes of everything that wasn't bolted down, but sadly seem to have given them all away! Anyway, it was a very grand way to arrive for our research visit and the omens felt good. We met a number of contacts from across the private client and investment spectrum and quickly concluded that our international perspective would be a clear differentiator and that our name and reputation would market well. We were also delighted that Smith Barney wanted to work with us and that they would offer our service through their packaged investment programme, called their ACE programme, which they distributed nationally. They were the perfect partner and once we had worked out the logistics of linking into their investment platform, we could manage the equity modules for their clients.

Over the months that followed, I made numerous trips to the US, covering the states from north to south and east to west.

It was great fun, an eye-opener in terms of cultural differences and economically worthwhile from the business we raised. It was on one visit to San Francisco, accompanied by Carol on this occasion, that we met Fritz Maytag, Carol's cousin, and so began the long overdue catch-up for her with a close family member that she had so missed in her childhood. We got along famously from the outset and include Fritz and his wife, Beverly, among our very closest family.

Life at MAM by the mid 1990s was steady, socially enjoyable and professionally fulfilling, and the investment track record remained strong. I had successfully transitioned from the Royal Marines and established myself as a valued member of the private client team. Importantly, I had begun to develop a valuable 'Rolodex' of contacts in the private client advisory community (lawyers, accountants, trustees, etc.) who would be vital to me as a quantifiable resource. But the situation at the investment bank, S.G. Warburg & Co., was considerably less certain and we began to see a steady exodus of talented individuals, which is never a good sign. The problem was the liberalisation of markets post-Big Bang and the arrival of the big international banks – US banks, in particular. It exposed SGW's relatively limited access to capital and the need for globally coordinated advice, issuance and trading. SGW needed a big global partner, but the very act of exploring such a merger can be destabilising and the senior directors failed to keep it secret, leading to a huge loss of investor confidence and a weakened negotiating position. SGW was swallowed by Swiss Bank Corporation and in the process it became clear that the real 'jewel in the SGW crown' was MAM's huge pension fund business.

MAM's future as a pure asset manager still looked very strong; however, what I mourned was the loss of our corporate broking and merchant banking colleagues, who provided the cross-disciplinary advice and support for so many of our clients, especially the booming entrepreneurial generation that was beginning to emerge. I began to realise that I wanted to be part of an international banking group rather than a pure asset manager and so began to look around for a new home.

Union Bank of Switzerland

I had some quite fixed opinions about which banks I wanted to meet and wrote off the US names as being too sales-oriented and aggressive, as well as the more regionally focused European ones. It left me looking specifically at the Swiss banks and I was delighted a few months later to accept an offer from Union Bank of Switzerland (UBS). I joined them in the summer of 1996 with a specific mandate to develop UK business. Switzerland had been the ultimate destination for private clients for centuries, where the famous Swiss Bank secrecy was still enshrined in law. Certainly, many clients were drawn simply because of its impenetrable shield from revenue authorities around the world and there were plenty of stories relating to Nazi gold and numbered accounts. However, the legacy of this somewhat convenient and self-serving proposition was gradually unravelling by the mid 1990s and the mainstream Swiss banks knew that they needed to develop a rather more competitive proposition than simply 'give us your money and we won't tell anyone', which seemed to have been the main message in the past. There was a steady international drive towards greater sharing of information between revenue authorities, and the bigger Swiss banks realised that they needed to build up domestic 'onshore' businesses to counter the huge revenue reliance on their 'offshore' business. My arrival was one of the early manifestations of this new domestic market initiative, even if there was a limit to what I would be able to achieve on my own!

One of the first things I found at UBS was that the doors

opened up a wider prospective client base for whom a global brand and banking services were equally important to pure investment and wealth management. In fact, the banking and convenience aspects often became the main drivers of interest, especially as this was reinforced by the still important element of Swiss bank security. I immediately reactivated my network of intermediaries and spent most of the next twelve months travelling around the country and the offshore centres, as well as the key London firms. I was rewarded with some big new mandates and felt certain that my move from MAM had been well timed.

However, after less than a year at UBS came the announcement that the bank was merging with Swiss Bank Corporation to form a new mega-bank UBS AG. The new UBS was a giant and, interestingly for me, reunited me with all my friends and connections at Warburg, which had been acquired by SBC a few years earlier. However, it quickly became clear that the SBC management team were dominant in the relationship with all the key appointments being taken by them. The SBC team were also much clearer in their goals for developing a global network of domestic private banking operations and the old UBS team were seen as too wedded to their traditional 'offshore' platforms. It was the recipe for somewhat divisive SBC versus UBS internal politics and a period of uncertainty before the chosen structure emerged. However, as far as the UK was concerned, it was a greenfield site as SBC had even less activity in London than UBS and I was selected to lead the new build-up of a UK domestic 'onshore' proposition.

The two to three years that followed were probably the most professionally interesting of my career, as well as the most challenging and politically difficult. The global head of the 'onshore' group was a truly exceptional man with visionary outlook on what was needed to transform UBS into a new global domestic banking powerhouse. He must have had at least 100 'brilliant ideas' every day, of which perhaps only a handful were realistic or practical, and he also had an unfortunate ability to antagonise and irritate as many people as he inspired. This was especially true of the older UBS 'offshore' bankers who were, in effect, being asked to finance this very expensive new business plan, knowing that in so doing it would undermine their own business and revenues. The 'onshore versus offshore' battle commenced and London was at the epicentre of this conflict, not least because of the very international nature of London's client base and the non-domiciled community in particular. 'Non-doms' enjoyed a very favourable regime at the time by being able to live in the UK, but provided they kept their assets offshore and the necessary rules were followed, they could avoid paying any UK tax on their offshore wealth. Unsurprisingly, the non-dom community in London was huge and a key target for banks, but it played directly into the ambiguity of the new UBS onshore and offshore communities.

One of my first challenges, however, was to build up a credible and senior team with products and services tailored for the UK market. As a newcomer to the domestic scene in the UK, we had to develop a completely fresh proposition that would maximise the benefits that we, as a global bank, could deliver in a local, relevant and tax-friendly way. It required some clear thinking around what clients wanted, what was already available in the market and how to differentiate our new proposition. We then had to ensure that we had the necessary capabilities, custody and reporting platforms, products, staffing, etc. needed to deliver this reliably. The early months were challenging yet very exciting, as we defined and shaped the new business and began to lay the foundations. I had to hire a team from scratch and over the course of the first eighteen months, I hired about forty-five bankers, organised into teams to tackle specific client segments (e.g. the executive community of high earners, business entrepreneurs, non-doms, etc.). It was a fascinating time and despite the inevitable snags and frustrations, we began to gain momentum and accumulate assets. My senior team were very much partners in this process and we developed a tight-knit and effective unit as we began to gain traction, despite the continuing political arrows being fired at us by the offshore group.

One highlight of those early years was the regular management offsite sessions. These were generally held in one of the various new domestic locations so, in turn, these were hosted in London, Paris, Frankfurt, Zurich and, more interestingly, Tokyo, where a new platform had been established to target the Far Eastern markets. Looking back, it does seem absurd that as head of the UK onshore business, I attended an offsite in Tokyo, but it made for a memorable trip and some very amusing experiences. When I heard that we would be heading out to Tokyo, I decided that Carol and I should make a proper trip out of it and add a few days' holiday each side of the event to visit the country. Accordingly, we planned an exciting itinerary for the four days before the meeting, including a visit to Kinugawa Onsen – one of the most famous of the numerous thermal bath resorts dotted around Japan.

Our adventure began at Tokyo Airport, which, although we didn't realise at the time, would be the last time we spoke English or saw any English signs for the following four days. We had to travel by train into Tokyo, change terminals and take another train onwards to Kinugawa. The first drama occurred on the train journey into Tokyo while we were relaxing and watching the countryside sliding by. A young Japanese girl walking towards me down the aisle suddenly collapsed unconscious at my feet, sending her handbag and its contents flying across the carriage. Initially, I was tempted with the typical British response of pretending not to notice, but quickly realised that I probably ought to try and help. I got her into the recovery position and tried to work out what might have happened. At that point, I looked around the carriage for some help, only to see a man rush out of the door and disappear. He returned with the guard a few minutes later just as the girl regained consciousness. It transpired that she had had an epileptic fit and was not the worse for wear. She disappeared with copious bowing and hand clasping – "*Arigato*! *Arigato*!" she said.

It seemed that our adventure had only started when we arrived in Tokyo and faced the subway connection to the outgoing station for Kinugawa. There was no English signage anywhere and we had to enlist the help of a deaf and dumb lady to work the ticket machine and find the platform. I am not quite sure how we ended up with a deaf mute, but she was very helpful! We arrived at the new terminal, but were still faced with a very long walk. In the era of unwheeled luggage, this prospect was daunting and I decided that I had to try and find some wheels before my arms became permanently stretched. I left Carol in an underground subway and, rather like Theseus and his ball of string in the Knossos labyrinth, headed out into the maze of Tokyo streets above. It was chaos, but I did eventually find a luggage shop and, even more surprisingly, two sets of luggage wheels. My mental arithmetic must have failed me (or else I was ripped off) as I later discovered that these two trolleys cost over £100 each! Carol was overwhelmingly happy to see me again after nearly an hour fending off strange characters in the subway and, with our luggage now more easily wheeled around, we set off again in high spirits.

The next challenge was in Kinugawa itself when we found ourselves in a deserted train station in the darkness with no taxi rank or any map to guide us. We resorted to wandering around the town centre clutching the fax confirmation of our booking, trying to match the Japanese symbols of the hotel name on the fax with the illuminated neon signs on the roofs. Comments like "It looks like a backwards 'E' with a funny bit at the top left" must have been comical to anyone listening!

With a huge sense of relief, we finally walked up to the front desk of our hotel after about forty-five minutes of wandering the streets, only to find that they spoke no English whatsoever. However, we were, at least, expected and were shown up to our room with much fussing and apparent delight by our giggling kimono-wearing attendants. The room resembled a school dojo with the same flooring and no visible furniture or bed. There was a small table no more than six inches high and various cushions scattered around. We were exhausted after travelling for some twenty-four hours and, after a light meal, quickly fell fast asleep despite the hard floor and no pillows! Our sleep lasted less than an hour before we were woken for our massages. Evidently, we had failed to distinguish am and pm properly and so underwent our morning massage at midnight, before finally allowing our pummelled and exhausted bodies to get some rest.

Everything in Japan was a novelty – from the food, the furniture (or lack of it), the language (which is incredibly alien) and the delight with which the locals treated us as if willing participants in some kind of ancient process of humiliation. But the prize must surely go to the Japanese bathing and lavatory rituals, which are unique. Since we were guests at an onsen, it was only expected that we should go bathing. We donned our kimonos and headed downstairs to the spa, where we discovered that male and female bathing is strictly segregated. I headed into my side to find various men who resembled off-duty sumo wrestlers steaming quietly in the bath. I decided to join them, but the water was so hot that it took several minutes and considerable determination to gradually lower myself in and I wondered if my 'wedding tackle' would ever be the same again. There then followed a period of gentle steaming, during which I began to take on the appearance of a 'boiled lobster', which is identified as such in the guest book, after which a break is recommended. I headed for the small stools against the walls where there were various taps and hoses. Once again, everything seemed to be six inches off the ground and very awkward to get at. The first tap I tried sent a jet of freezing water directly into my genitals, provoking a scream of surprise and several disapproving looks from the sumo gang, still simmering gently in the bath. Eventually, I worked it out and was able to rinse off and head back to the room. The next novelty were the lavatories, which in Japan are much more than simple porcelain receptacles. The loos were properly multifunctional and could play music and spray water at your nether regions, with fans to dry you off – and, in fact, could help you do almost everything. I had great fun playing with all the settings to ensure that when it was Carol's turn, she would experience an intense and very intimate cold jet in that most private of places. Her scream a few minutes later informed me that I had got it spot on!

We decided that we wanted to go for a walk after our adventures in the spa and bathroom, and I composed a long phrase from our phrase book to ask: 'Where is the best place for us to see Mount Fuji?' I went downstairs to deliver this carefully prepared sentence to the receptionist, mindful that I probably wouldn't understand his answer. But his reaction was even more bizarre. He rushed into his office and I could hear lots of chattering and giggling from his assistant, before he re-emerged with a large map of Japan. He then proceeded to tell me in pidgin English about the four-hour train ride and one-hour taxi ride needed to get to Mount Fuji, which was at the other end of the huge map he tried to unravel for me. He must have thought I was mad and certainly his giggling assistant was highly entertained. Well, so much for my belief that we were in a hotel near Mount Fuji and we settled for a short walk around the town instead.

When we eventually joined up with the other UBS team in Tokyo a few days later, we had plenty of stories to share and, to this day, we laugh about that trip and all the funny things that happened. Shoes are always taken off indoors and I recall having to use a felt pen to blacken someone's toe when he realised his sock had a hole in it; there was also confusion about whether shoes should be placed facing or away from the door (one is highly disrespectful, indicating the desire for a speedy getaway); and there is a whole etiquette of sneezing – Carol unfortunately had a sneezing fit that seemed to agitate one local restaurant enormously! As for the offsite, I can't even remember what we discussed!

Back in London, life continued in earnest and we were flat out for client pitches and winning mandates. I was very pleased in early 2000 to be promoted to managing director in the annual review and it seemed that I was in the right place at the right time with an effective team, some great colleagues and growing momentum. But I wasn't blind to our big cost base and knew that we needed to accelerate our revenues if we were to deflect the continuing pressure and resentment from the offshore group. What I did not know was that the costs and build out of the new domestic businesses around the world was being questioned at main board level, and management changes were coming.

A few months later, at one of the regular management conferences in Basel, all the country heads were asked to bring their key management teams with them and we were collectively informed that the global head of the domestic businesses was stepping down. It was a huge surprise as it was his vision, energy and support at group level that had brought us so far forwards and placed UBS firmly on the map in key domestic locations. It seemed like a last gasp challenge by the remaining offshore regime to restore their primacy and, suddenly, we faced structural and reporting changes that threatened all the momentum we had been building. Over the course of the next six months, each country head in turn was replaced and reporting lines changed. Although both the heads of Italy and Spain went a few weeks before me, I was nonetheless nonplussed when I was called in to be told that my career at UBS was over. It seemed so arbitrary and unfair and I was devastated, having never experienced this type of behaviour. I was totally unprepared for such a personal blow. What was galling was that we had laid the foundations of a substantial long-term business for the bank in London, and after a brief change in strategy, the bank reverted to broadly the same approach as we had originally adopted. It is noteworthy that the domestic business at UBS now comprises several hundred bankers across multiple UK locations, but the original nucleus was the team I built and in that I take great pride.

So now what? The stock market was recovering from the tech crash in 2000 and school fees were starting to bite, so I needed to get focused and find a new job. It took some time to recover from the shock of events and, on a personal level, it was quite a struggle, but I began to gain some leads. Towards the end of 2000, I was in final discussions with the London-based arm of Alex Brown, the brokerage business, that had just been acquired by Deutsche Bank. I liked the Alex Brown model and, in particular, their focus on entrepreneurial wealth and the high-earning executive community. I had met the management team in Baltimore and was just about to sign when the European head of Deutsche Private Bank called to ask me to work with him in integrating the Alex Brown business into the UK platform of Deutsche Bank, which was also trying to consolidate the old Morgan Grenfell private client business and the Bankers Trust team, all of which had been accumulated by the group over preceding years. It looked messy and, indeed, proved to be so, but at the time I felt I needed the job and I probably failed to read the tea leaves properly on what was always going to be a big cultural challenge.

Deutsche Bank

Having experienced the fickle and exposed nature of being a 'non-revenue earning senior manager', I made sure I had a tight contract with a ring-fenced bonus entitlement just in case things went pear-shaped again for reasons outside my control. What a sensible precaution it proved to be. I had been at the bank for less than a month when the person who hired me, the head of the European Private Bank, was moved on and I realised that there were some intractable problems and a fundamental lack of strategic direction. The global head of private banking seemed to be distracted by multiple domestic challenges in Germany and I was left to try and resolve the integration of the Alex Brown brokerage team within the London platform. Furthermore, I had to try and defend an attempt by the chairman of the asset management business to close down the Jersey bank and trust company, which were vital elements of the proposition we needed in London to serve our UK and international client base. His reasoning was that he needed cash to pay the annual bonus round in London! Being confronted with so many fundamental challenges to the operation of the London private bank, I took the view that I should either resign then and there (less than three months into the job) or stick to my principles and fight for what I felt was needed. I decided on the latter and immediately lent my support to the offshore bank and trust business, earning their gratitude and friendship, as well as embarking on a restructuring of the London team.

The restructuring was well overdue given how the team had grown over the previous few years and there was considerable 'slack' in the headcount and organisation. This is management code for the need for redundancies and over the course of the next three months, I had to lay off about fifteen staff, mainly in the operations department. Having been through this exact process myself only a year earlier, I knew exactly how they felt and the hollowness of words at such moments. However, I believe that these cases were all handled fairly and were properly justified. The greater challenge I was facing was trying to integrate the brokers and the somewhat self-centred broking culture of the Alex Brown team within the private bank – a task that should really have been handled at group management level, not locally by me. It created a pretty toxic environment in London and I felt that whatever I did, I was managing to upset someone. What was frustrating was the fact that I believed that, if properly focused and supported, Deutsch Bank was well placed to make progress in London. It was a well-capitalised bank, had a good array of products and services, and there were some excellent fund managers in the team. The problem was constant stop-start strategic thinking and a turnover of senior staff.

One tragic but memorable day occurred on 11th September that year – 9/11. I was in a meeting at CAPCO, a management consultancy being run by my old boss from UBS, discussing the restructuring of my team, when a secretary rushed in to tell us that a plane had hit one of the twin towers in New York. We assumed it was a Cessna or similar and thought what a dreadful accident. It was only when I got back to my office that I watched, aghast, as the second passenger jet hit the other tower and the enormity of the tragedy unfolded in Manhattan. Carol and I had been in that same building only a few years earlier for a meeting and so I was familiar with the size and scale of the place. For the Deutsche Bank team, it was tragically close to home as their New York headquarters was directly opposite and some of the Alex Brown broking team had close friends (in one case, a fiancée) in the Cantor Fitzgerald office, which was on one of the floors above where the plane hit. That day saw a series of frantic phone calls with friends and loved ones, but tragically all of the Cantor team perished. Sitting under the shadow of the NatWest tower in the City, we suddenly became concerned about a copycat hit and decided to vacate and head home, reflecting on a very sad day. A few months later, I met a friend who had been in the World Financial Centre next door and she told me of the drama on the ground that day. She had been evacuated into Battery Park after the first tower collapsed. Lying on the ground as the second tower came down, they had debris raining down around them and one poor woman close by was killed by a large window that was catapulted away from the site and hit her.

All in all, it was a mixed and rather difficult period, but as I approached the end of my first year, I could point to some significant achievements. The offshore bank and trust company had been protected; we had established a booking platform and administrative support for the London team; I had completed the integration of the Alex Brown and Bankers Trust teams; and we had moved into refurbished new offices with far better working and breakout facilities. Overall, I felt that, notwithstanding the challenges remaining, I had delivered on what was asked of me. The next step, however, proved one too many. The European head was again replaced and I found myself with the third new boss in less than a year. Having to bring this person up to speed on all the evolutions of the previous year was a challenge, but it was soon clear that he did not share my vision for how London could become the lead European hub (ex-Germany) and that, as such, it needed supporting. To the contrary, he wanted me to reduce the London headcount from forty down to about fifteen and refocus our activities alongside the investment bank. I remember being at the Global Business Leaders' conference in New York when this new plan for London was proposed and I had a strong sense of déjà vu about how this would all end. A month or so later, while fighting another battle for the Jersey Trust business, I got the call from HR to go and see them and knew immediately what was up. I decided to keep them waiting while I packed up all my personal files and key papers and was just glad that I had negotiated a good bonus with which to exit. I gave a twenty-minute goodbye speech to the team, who I think were genuinely sorry to see me go, but I had been fighting someone or something almost every step of the way since I arrived and it was quite a relief to step down.

Strategic rethink and reflection

At the age of forty-five, I now faced a rethink about what I should do. I had transitioned from the RM and taken on two senior level management roles, but found that these had proved less rewarding than I expected. In particular, I realised that simply championing a business proposition, developing a strategy, and maximising the client service and experience was only part of the challenge for management. Successful long-term managers within a big bureaucratic organisation like a bank, have to manage the ambiguity of unsatisfactory situations and deflect or postpone difficult issues and generally 'go with the corporate flow'. It seemed to me that to play this role effectively required an almost ongoing acceptance of compromise and personal principles that could be adapted to suit the needs of the company. I have seen plenty of managers who had 'sold their souls' to their corporate master and I didn't want to go down this road. I also wanted to return closer to the source of client service and revenues, and avoid the 'non-revenue earning' tag that makes many managers vulnerable. I began to explore various family office teams, including some newly emerging multi-family offices, which were becoming popular with families who did not have enough money for a dedicated team of their own, but wanted a more personal and tailored approach than many private banks were able to deliver. I was also interested in the idea of a start-up business where I could shape a new proposition from the ground up and potentially make some real money. Building the UBS team had given me a taste for shaping strategy and developing the people and resources to deliver a new proposition. It was therefore very opportune that I took a call from a former UBS colleague, SAM Lusty, from the derivatives group, to explore a new idea he was working on.

Ryes Capital

SAM (we called him 'Sam', but really it was just his initials, hence the capital letters) saw an opportunity to develop a risk management platform with which to oversee allocations to hedge funds. The proliferation of hedge funds over the preceding decade had been phenomenal, with almost any self-respecting trader or manager keen to set up shop and develop a new strategy to target market inefficiencies, macro theories or trading opportunities. These funds were effectively unconstrained investment funds where managers could follow their conviction and exploit market inefficiencies, trading anomalies and multiple niche strategies. Some of the early managers were indeed outstanding and assets grew rapidly, as investors saw the freedom and potential outsize returns that could be made. It didn't take long for the charging structures of these funds to inflate and encourage other, often less gifted, managers to enter this arena.

Annual management fees of two per cent of the fund value plus a twenty per cent performance fee (two and twenty structures) soon became the norm. Many of these funds also used significant leverage to increase the returns they made and this could carry considerable additional risks (as well as potential returns) for investors. In theory, such funds should have been relatively uncorrelated – that is to say, the risk and return characteristics of each fund should have been quite independent of each other. However, the 2000 stock market collapse, driven by the collapse of technology stocks (the dot.com crash), had seen most hedge funds suffer across the board, which clearly indicated the failure of their hedging strategies and ultimately the similarity of their risk and return characteristics. In 1998, there had also been a spectacular crash at Long Term Capital Management, a 'black box' investment strategy, which had to be bailed out with $3.5 billion to stave off a banking crisis, and clients quite rightly became increasingly distrustful of the opacity of many hedge funds.

There appeared to be an opportunity to develop a platform where investors could identify the skills being demonstrated by the managers, together with an understanding of the associated risks. This would include an understanding of the impact of leverage. For example, two managers might produce a fifteen per cent performance return over a given period, but achieve this very differently. One could have achieved this by simply mirroring the relevant market index (beta returns), but then leveraged the return to achieve a fifteen per cent performance; while the other manager might have had no leverage, but achieved the performance through outstanding stock selection or trading excellence (alpha). Most investors would prefer the latter. Our plan was to map the hedge fund community and try and identify consistent patterns in how returns were being achieved and provide an advisory platform. Furthermore, we planned to use our insights into the 'alpha generators' to capture this 'alpha' and sell it as a specific product to institutions and banks. This, in a nutshell, was the Ryes Capital value proposition.

It was an institutional proposition that required us to convince two key participants of the value of our platform. First was the client, who needed to believe that the insights we could provide were unavailable elsewhere and, by having real-time visibility of the hedge fund trading positions, we could offer a genuine analysis of the relevant risks and/or even develop 'alpha-capture' and 'alpha-transport' products. At the same time, we needed to persuade the hedge funds that we had identified substantial institutional client interest to justify them opening up a managed account on our platform and manage a cloned version of their fund across a separate custody account. It was the latter that was essential in providing us with the real-time visibility of their trading and hence our ability to run risk metrics and analysis. All this was going to take time and money to establish and we needed an investor who would understand the proposition and be prepared to provide the working capital to get there. After searching a number of potential partners, I introduced Michael Spencer of ICAP, the leading UK inter-dealer broker, who agreed to fund us. It was a big bet on us by Spencer and we knew we had to deliver.

Since I didn't have the hedge fund or risk background to contribute to the technical proposition, I focused my skills on client acquisition and the day-to-day management of the business, leaving SAM to develop the maths and risk models. I become the Chief Operating Officer, managing the premises, cash, payroll and later headed the discussions with our chosen administrator and third-party custodian. What was unfortunate was that many of the individuals SAM brought in on the technical side were not team players, had competing egos and, surprisingly, were not as good as they thought themselves to be. It was a difficult atmosphere, but the longer we stuck at it, the more we began to believe that we could actually succeed. The key step forward was to build the managed account platform with an independent administrator and custodian. This we achieved in Dublin using EU/Irish umbrella fund laws to achieve a platform of ten sub-funds with independent management agreements with the hedge funds. We called the platform HedgeMAP and trademarked it. This was the culmination of nearly three years of hard work, long hours, expensive lawyers and administrators, but it also resulted in our first real engagement with an end-user client. The client was a substantial US life insurance group who liked the risk-managed approach to this asset class and the potential to moderate their own balance sheet risks. They committed to funding the platform with $250 million subject to agreeing paperwork and discussing mechanics and timing. This was an electrifying moment for the business and completely validated SAM's original vision and all the work we had orchestrated to make it happen. Tragically, though, this news caused the partnership to fragment with many of the newer partners suddenly squabbling about their respective equity interests in the business and who was really creating value. Although we had detailed shareholder agreements with all our colleagues – SAM and I had even invested a chunk of our own money – everything was thrown out of the window in a selfish melee of greed. It was the end of the dream and the glue that held us together began to dissolve.

It was, therefore, sadly inevitable that in all the stress and internally focused distraction, our crucial first key client withdrew their commitment to fund the platform. After that, things unravelled fast and those who had been squabbling for a bigger percentage saw all the value of the business rapidly slipping away. It was so short-sighted and frustrating, and to this day I cannot believe the self-defeating, self-centred and destructive way certain partners behaved, and the prize that slipped through our fingers as a result. It was another valuable, if rather painful, lesson in human behaviour and, in particular, the behaviour of the untamed capital markets banker!

As sad as it was, however, I was glad to have had a proper go at building a new business from scratch. It had been a huge learning curve and I realised how close the distinction is between success and failure. I now have enormous respect for entrepreneurs who live so close to the edge in their pursuit of a new business – we, too, had been so close to pulling this off. How valuable such a platform would have been during the 2008 financial crash! However, I now needed a job and preferably one that would pay me lots of money, as I had dug deep into savings over the previous three years with school fees peaking for all three children. I reached out to friends and contacts, as well as headhunters, and began to interview.

J.P. Morgan

I joined the private bank at J.P. Morgan in June 2005 as a managing director with responsibility to build out the UK client base and take on some of the major existing clients. It was my first hands-on client role for almost ten years and free from management responsibilities for a change. I thought it might be a fresh start, although having so little say in management issues did start to grate quite quickly. J.P. Morgan liked to put people in boxes with labels on them and I was in one which said 'Banker', not 'Manager'! However, it was a job and right then I needed to repair the family finances. It was also fortunate for me that the bank had just lost three ex-Flemings bankers and needed to pick up momentum quickly. Surprisingly, for such a global brand, J.P. Morgan's UK business was quite small, despite having acquired the Flemings business a few years earlier. Much of that business had been for quite small accounts, opened ironically by wealthy clients who simply wanted the rather smart Flemings cheque book! The Americans didn't really understand this and just wanted to focus on bigger accounts (10 million dollars or more). They were in the middle of clearing out these smaller accounts when I arrived – a process that was destroying so much goodwill with many very wealthy individuals that it was almost criminal! The result was that we lost the potential to cross market to a deep existing client base and had to start from scratch. I was also surprised how ill-equipped we were with no Sterling-denominated model investment portfolios, no tax-compliant mutual funds or tax reporting package. It was a similar situation to the one I had to address at UBS over seven years earlier.

However, I quickly discovered that the cachet of the J.P. Morgan brand name was valuable and there was a presumptive quality behind everything we did. One of my first tasks was to host a major tax and investment conference at Villa d'Este on Lake Como in Italy. Such a chore, as you can imagine! The attendees were largely drawn from the lawyers and accountants I had got to know so well when I was at Mercury Asset Management and so it was something of a reunion, as well as a great chance to reconnect and explain my hopes for building the J.P. Morgan business. The guest speaker, who I introduced for the main gala dinner, was William Hague MP, who gave a wonderfully funny speech and we all flew home the following day in high spirits after three glorious days in the Italian sunshine. Carol was terribly envious of my five-star suite overlooking the lake and my spin around the lake in a Riva, trying to work out which was George Clooney's villa.

I look back on my time at J.P. Morgan being in two very clear halves. The first half being before the 2008 financial market crash. This was a period of exciting growth and some major client acquisition. The previous banker team were sitting on substantial assets and were evidently less proactive in banging on doors and finding new clients. They had also not really tried to build up the requisite products to support a broader UK client push. As part of a new team of bankers, my arrival coincided with a wave of new accounts and I spent the first six to twelve months working hard to build out the Sterling product suite and relevant services. The net result was that we began to develop real momentum and started to win a significant number of new accounts and the key intermediary community regarded us as a safe pair of hands combined with a great brand. It felt like we were in the right place at the right time with a brand that stood out. The recent acquisition of the Cazenove investment banking business also created significant traction with UK entrepreneurial businesses, leading to a closer integration with the investment bank, harking back to the good old days at Warburg.

One of the early highlights was a week-long induction visit to the 'mothership' in New York. It is only in the US that you can appreciate the scale of the Chase / J.P. Morgan brand with a branch on almost every street corner. It is a huge institution, making the London office seem a rather quaint backwater by comparison. The machinery that supported the bankers was also very comprehensive, especially all the financial planning and wealth structuring, and we started to learn how to use this resource even though it was very US-centric. It was quickly obvious that the overall quality and backgrounds of employees was very impressive. Most were from good families and all shared a strong work ethic and determination to succeed. It was a very positive environment and in some respects reminded me of the pursuit of excellence both in the Royal Marines and then latterly at Mercury Asset Management. When you witness it, you recognise it, and there are few institutions that pull this off as well as J.P. Morgan.

My highlight at J.P. Morgan and perhaps my entire private banking career was winning one mega deal that was, at the time, the single biggest new client ever signed up by the bank – $4.6 billion. Ironically, it was through my old boss at UBS, who sat on the family board of a Swiss-based pharmaceutical firm that cashed out for c$10 billion and needed to park some of the cash pending redeployment. Winning the chance to pitch for the deal was harder than I had realised with a sharp-elbowed banker in New York claiming a closer connection. However, it soon became clear that they wanted me and I led the pitch team, together with the global head of asset management, the head of the fixed income group and wealth-structuring group. We spent weeks assembling the documents responding to their 'Request for Proposal' (RFP) and several iterations later we were shortlisted to meet the principal and his board in Geneva. It was just before Christmas 2006 and we waited with bated breath to hear whether we would be successful. They took ages to respond, by which time we were all on holiday in Klosters and I recall reading the email on my BlackBerry heading up the Schwarzseealp chair lift. I nearly dropped the phone and couldn't wait to share the news. However, as exciting as this was, I also knew that these funds would only be held temporarily with us as they would be redeployed into a series of new businesses. So, during the course of 2007, my client statistics showed a record inflow, followed by a record outflow! But we made some good money en route for both the client and the bank, and it was an important way to get myself on the map within the private bank.

Shortly after this big win, I was asked to join the bank's Advisory Council, which composed the key bankers across the bank. It was an honour and also a good way to meet the management hierarchy in New York and elsewhere. We had some valuable conferences and shared best practice ideas around the world. However, it seemed to me that buying into the party line was a big part of the council's purpose and while the engine in the US was well developed and efficient, the needs of key international centres like London were not given the same priorities and some key differences were not properly understood. This is, perhaps, where the seeds of frustration began to develop and despite the rapid accumulation of clients and assets during the pre-liquidity crash of 2008, my UK boss proved unwilling to champion some of the changes that I felt were needed to reinforce the London platform and our international credentials.

The 2008 banking crisis was a dramatic 'Bonfire of the Vanities' and was the first time I had watched real stress hit markets – far worse that the 1987 correction or the UK ERM exit in the early 1990s. It also proved to be a spectacular opportunity for J.P. Morgan, whose balance sheet strength and very strict risk-management protocols proved to be a winning combination. It was very upsetting to hear stories of bankers at Bear Stearns and then Lehman Brothers lose everything – their jobs, all their deferred bonuses and, in many cases, their accumulated wealth. Share prices collapsed and expressions such as 'catching a falling knife' exemplified the risks of trying to buy collapsing stocks. I did buy some J.P. Morgan shares at $19, but missed on really 'filling up' at $15. Today's share price is in excess of $150! Isn't hindsight cruel?

As impressive as the bank was in terms of its stability and strength, the real legacy of the 2008 crash was a wave of compulsive risk management and excessive supervision that swept through management. So determined was the group to avoid losses or reputational issues that it became obsessive about covenants and procedures, and several clients who were struggling to manage the fallout of the crisis were treated unnecessarily harshly. One major client of mine had borrowed against his company's shares and unfortunately the value of these fell through two margin call levels on one day. His business was still very well supported, but in the light of the Lehman bankruptcy, no risks were to be tolerated and I had to visit the client and his wife in a London restaurant to get him to pledge the art in his New York apartment as additional collateral. Client loyalty and appreciation get sorely tested on such occasions and his other main banker adopted a far more accommodating approach that proved hugely embarrassing and made me realise that a 'take no prisoners' approach to private banking was probably not a sensible strategy.

What we began to see during 2009 and beyond was increasing micro-management of our activities in London and this marked what I now see as the second 'half' of my time with the bank. Whereas the earlier years had been relatively unconstrained and entrepreneurial, it seemed that we were constantly under the spotlight, at a time when new business flows were also challenging and we were not seen to be living up to our previous reputation. Perhaps because of our early success, London was seen as the new growth hotspot, but without any real understanding of what was needed to deliver success there. Some changes were needed strategically and yet the pressure was relentlessly on product sales and centralised investment solutions. It was all about selling and less about service, and with this change came a period of decreasing satisfaction and enjoyment.

The other facet of change was the introduction of a much more comprehensive personal qualification, investment suitability and risk-management agenda, which required a huge amount of new paperwork and client confirmation. Quite rightly, the industry wanted to protect investors, especially the basic retail investor on the high street, from unscrupulous advisers, but the result very quickly became a minefield of compliance requirements that became more and more restrictive to the larger investment portfolios and more sophisticated private banking clients. Unfortunately, the rules applied to all private individuals unless a client elected to 'opt up' to an institutional relationship, which then removed certain protections. We had to reaffirm every relationship and ensure that advice was being, and had been, given appropriately. As you can imagine, it was not a popular pastime and encroached on active new client initiatives, much to everyone's frustration. The other element was the need for all advisers to sit and pass a level six exam (degree level) in Private Client Investment Advice and Management ('PCIAM'). Apart from the various multiple-choice US regulatory exams I had sat in the early 1990s, all my UK credentials had been acquired 'on the job' with internal certification being provided for the necessary regulatory bodies. This was rather quaintly called being 'grandfathered'. The new PCIAM exam was a serious, three-hour written paper and presented bankers across the City with major pangs of anxiety and self-doubt. I hadn't sat a three-hour written exam for over thirty years! The course included three modules: investment management and advisory concepts, UK tax, and derivatives. The first two were fairly straightforward, having been my 'bread and butter' for many years, but the derivatives module was quite a challenge. I spent literally hours revising (far more than the course said was needed), but – what a relief – I passed first go and could then amuse myself watching other unfortunate senior MDs face up to the same stresses.

It was ironic to some extent that the new regulatory environment provided the perfect excuse for banks to refocus their services away from the broader and more flexible propositions of old and provide much narrower guidelines for clients, thereby ensuring that there were fewer exceptions to monitor and that greater standardisation of advice could be applied in portfolio construction and oversight. While it can certainly be argued that the core investment convictions of a bank should suit all clients seeking the same overall outcome, inevitably this discards the nuance of individual circumstances, timing, tax and other historic constraints, and it gradually commoditises the service on offer. However, it was a strategy that suited senior management at a time of heightened internal risks, and the role of bankers providing more personalised advice and service gradually became replaced with product-centric selling and sales targets. It wasn't a great evolution to my mind and further reinforced the shift of many wealthy families towards the establishment of their own independent family offices and 'so-called' multi-family offices, although the latter were really little more than new private banks and many have succumbed to the same pressures and priorities.

My work gradually began to shift towards the family office community and individuals with very substantial assets. Such needs inevitably straddled both investment management issues, but also capital raising, corporate advice, tax and succession planning, and next generation education. It was very fulfilling to work with clients across the full range of their affairs, rather than simply their investment needs, and we developed a multi-centre servicing proposition with Geneva, New York and Singapore, combining to provide a global perspective. Ultimately, though, J.P. Morgan wanted all the wallet share and this was simply not realistic. Furthermore, the acquisition time for these huge clients was much longer than regular client pitches and the growth progression of the UHNW team was inevitably very lumpy and uncertain. At the same time as targeting the ultra-rich, the bank was also considering venturing into the mainstream private banking area, by which it meant clients of investment portfolios of around $5m. This was a much more commoditised proposition, but was arguably a better level at which to pitch into the UK market; and although I could see the dangers of confusing our image by having two different propositions, I decided to throw my hat into the ring to lead this new group, as I hoped to be able to finesse the implementation of the strategy by knowing my way around the group and my understanding of the choke points.

I didn't win the role, but I welcomed the new head into her role with a genuinely meant 'good luck', knowing how difficult her task would be. She lasted three years and then moved on, having run into all the issues (and more) that I had feared. By then, I was well on my way mentally to a new project, namely to try and develop a cross-disciplinary advisory proposition that would appeal to very wealthy families, especially those running businesses, where capital raising, corporate advice, tax, succession and a myriad of other elements all need to be coordinated. Essentially, it was a return to the more holistic thinking that existed in the old S.G. Warburg days.

Edmond de Rothschild Private Merchant Banking

The name we devised said it all. Private merchant banking reflected the post-war thinking of the old British banks and embraced an advice-led proposition where a bank would assemble its skills and services around a client to find the best outcome. It required a different mix of skills and a longer-term perspective on the payoff. I was part of a new team assembled by an old UBS friend of mine who, in turn, brought in former colleagues and friends from Goldman Sachs, Hawkpoint (a corporate advisory boutique), Lehman and J.P. Morgan. I also brought a CIO and other portfolio-management expertise, and very quickly we assembled a team that shared our vision for a new service proposition. That we were able to persuade one of Europe's most prestigious banking names to back us was hugely valuable and we began the task of building out a new London operation that would tap into the existing infrastructure and capabilities of the group elsewhere.

It was a very exciting start, as all new ventures are, with passions and energy high and a desire for success underpinning everyone and everything. We had a spectacular launch party at Lancaster House, conducted various roadshows around Europe and began to generate both client interest and momentum in our new approach. However, it didn't take long for us to realise that the group was facing some major stresses. A generation of older divisional heads were leaving; the onset of European banking rules was beginning to impact important revenue models; and, last but not least, the acceleration of sentiment and legislation against tax evasion and undeclared assets was ferocious. As with many other Swiss banks we soon discovered that there were several such accounts representing a valuable element of the group's business. This created a difficult time for the new team in London as we had painted a picture of a new business model targeting the sophisticated family office and entrepreneur market, and management expectations were high. We had set ourselves a tough task to establish a completely new regulated platform (which we set up as a partnership with the Rothschild family), including administrative and trading infrastructure, reporting and banking tools, and essentially a whole new wealth-management machine. Dealing with these teething issues as well as finding new clients proved to be a race against time.

We had agreed a five-year arrangement after which the family could buy out our partnership interests and absorb the business into their bank directly. We had negotiated a very good deal with the family when we joined, perhaps too good, and this put pressure on us to deliver. The nature of a broader, cross-disciplinary service, however, was that big revenues are lumpy and irregular, and the bank was more used to the steady revenues from assets under management, (AuM). We had some major successes and were on the cusp of closing two major corporate advisory deals worth $2m plus in our third year when we partners were called into a special meeting one evening with management. The head of the London branch, who had assembled our team, had been sacked a week earlier, so the omens didn't bode well. We were informed that the bank wanted to wind up our partnership and absorb it into the regular bank. It was frustratingly short-sighted given the momentum of business that was growing. However, it was clear that the vacuum of senior management caused by the retirement of most of the old guard, together with the pressures of new regulations and collapsing revenues, was driving the family into a corner and there was a dramatic culling of costs around Europe.

It was incredibly sad as well as frustrating, not least because most of us were senior bankers and saw this as the last major career opportunity before retiring. To leave now with so much value 'on the table' seemed ridiculous, but we were stuck.

Looking back on these events now, the major issue could well have been the attractiveness of the deal we had originally struck with the bank when we set up the partnership. All those who had signed off on this deal had left shortly after we arrived; the new senior management team were unconvinced with what we could deliver and were patently jealous of the financial cushion we had negotiated for ourselves. I took the view that none of us would have joined without such a 'cushion', but this was largely immaterial as we collected our belongings and left the bank. The immediate decision was 'what next?'.

Plural Life

Being unemployed was not a new experience, but being deprived of doing something that I really believed in was incredibly frustrating. It was also impossible to do without an institution behind me. The partners discussed whether we should try and rebuild the business elsewhere and we had conversations with a variety of other small banks and asset managers to explore how we might do so. In the end, three of the partners formed a new corporate advisory business and indeed went on to pick up some of the transactions that Rothschild had discarded, and they are now doing quite well. The others and most of the staff decided to stay with Rothschild, but I didn't want to stay, particularly in light of the decision to 'pull the rug' on our business just as it was starting to gain traction.

It was at this rather inopportune moment that my health decided to play up and, following a bout of septicaemia, I discovered that my heart had been damaged and was no longer pumping blood around my body as effectively as it should. I discovered this the hard way when I fainted on two consecutive days, one time when I was on the top table at a Goldsmiths' Livery Company dinner, much to the concern of the Prime Warden sitting next to me! I don't intend to dwell on this, but suffice to say that it did take my eye off the ball of looking for a new job and instead made me focus on the things that were more important to me, namely Carol, the family and my friends. It also prompted me to write this book.

I didn't stop looking for a new job altogether, though. Instead, it made me look harder at what I really enjoyed doing as opposed to all those other things that I had done simply because they went with a particular job. Having just turned sixty, I also thought that it was time for me to reprioritise my life for a change. Of course, the normal pressures for going back to work are financial, and with bank and savings accounts somewhat depleted after school fees, weddings and the general costs of living, not to mention the upkeep at Bottom Farm, I was conscious that doing nothing wasn't a realistic option either. I needed to make some money to keep the general finances afloat, but, more importantly, I wanted to keep my brain engaged and active and, where possible, to use the knowledge and contacts I had built up over the last thirty years in a constructive way. This effectively meant an advisory or fundraising role of some description, and/or a non-executive directorship with a family business or wealth manager where I could immediately add value.

And so began a plural life with multiple irons in the fire and different initiatives with former colleagues and clients. Since this is the life I am currently leading, it seems a sensible place to draw together my work-time reflections, but I will just conclude with two important roles that have been running in the background, and to which I am now devoting more meaningful time. The first of these, which will keep me focused for a few years yet to come, is my role with the Goldsmiths' Company. This livery company is one of the 'Great Twelve' such companies in the City, being the ancient medieval guilds of London. Receiving its Royal Charter in 1327, the Goldsmiths' Company is the fifth oldest and, as its name suggests, was one of the leading institutions in the City during the days when gold and silver were the key commodities for banking transactions. It still retains responsibility for ensuring the standards of gold and silver, and the assaying and hallmarking (literally the marking of items in the Hall) continues to this day. The company also checks the nation's coinage on an annual basis to make sure there has been no tampering or reduction in the various metal constituents. This check became formalised as the Trial of the Pyx and continues to this day with coins being counted, assayed and checked against Royal Mint records. It is an extraordinarily archaic tradition, but, in the days when tampering with legal tender was punishable with castration (among other gruesome fates), it reminds one of the power such institutions had 700 years ago!

My connection to the Goldsmiths' Company was through the Pixley family and I was absolutely delighted to be invited to join them by Cousin Ti (Pixley), my father's first cousin. The Pixley family had been in the bullion business for many years and Great Uncle Stewart had been the Prime Warden of the Goldsmiths' Company in the late nineteenth century. Being able to carry on the family tradition in the company was therefore very special. I joined first as a Freeman in 1997 and was then elected a Liveryman in 2009. I was already, by then, a member of the investment committee, which also proved to be a valuable complement to my private banking conversations, giving me additional perspectives on managers, markets and long-term investing. In 2017, I was elected as an assistant to the Court (effectively the board of the company) and this means that, in due course, I will expect to become Prime Warden, which maps out a valuable role for me over the next fifteen to twenty years. It has been a rich and interesting time, and both Carol and I have met some fascinating and unusual people through the company. It is also clear that being part of a valid and active ongoing trade, the Goldsmiths' Company is much more grounded than many of the other livery companies whose trades have long since disappeared and they have simply become charitable institutions.

The other role to which I am now devoting more time is as a trustee of the Clocktower Foundation (the charity that supports the serving soldiers and their families of 22 SAS Regiment) and the SBS Association. Despite not having served with the SBS, my introduction and continuing connections with the Special Forces community through friends and former colleagues has ensured that I have remained close ever since. It seems entirely appropriate, therefore, to give something back, both financially and with my time, for the debt I owe personally to the SBS for helping shape my military career, as well as the broader debt owed by the country to this very small but truly dedicated group of soldiers, who operate around the world, normally unseen and unknown, to protect our interests and freedoms.

The very nature of Special Forces activities precludes normal public fundraising activities and yet, given the non-stop tempo of commitments, these soldiers as well as their families often need much more support than most regular units, be that surgery or rehabilitation from injury, mental health and PTSD issues, or family difficulties. Visits to Stirling Lines in Hereford or the Royal Marines camp at Poole regularly reminds me of the extraordinary nature and scope of SF activities and yet the remarkably unassuming and humble nature of those involved. It is always a privilege to meet these people and my work as a trustee and association member is immensely rewarding.

The net result of working on multiple projects for multiple people is that my time seems to be in as short supply as ever, but at least it is my own to allocate. This has given me far greater freedom to fit other things into my day and to start considering the longer retired years ahead. However, I still carry my old working disciplines with me, so it is certainly not a life of hedonistic enjoyment and free time... at least not yet! Quite the opposite, in fact, with the continuous pressure of not wanting to let people down. Working flat out on any project I give myself is the only way I know how to operate and I see no reason to change things now.

UBS lures Madeley from MAM

UBS's private banking operation has decided to tackle the UK domestic market and hired Richard Madeley (above) from Mercury Asset Management, which manages in excess of £16bn of private client money.

Madeley, 39, who had been UK marketing director in the private client division, says he had long been surprised that UBS had not been operating in his patch.

One of the attractions of the UBS job, says Madeley, is the fact that private banking is "the heritage of the group, it lies at the core of its business". He also admits that his career path was blocked at MAM.

Joining at vice president level, Madeley plans to develop business both with UK residents and with those "who look to the UK for tax avoidance schemes".
Katharine Campbell

On the move

Parkin flies in to Bristol

■ John Parkin is moving Bristol to become manag director of its airport, ow by the city council. Park who is 42 and has held management posts at Thomas Cook and P&O, succeeds Peter Clayson, is taking early retirement At the same time, Mike Luddy is leaving Gatwick airport to be Bristol's marketing director.

Bristol airport handled 1.49m passengers and ma record pre-tax profits of £5.2m in the last financia year. Parkin takes over a time when the city counc considering options for private investment in a

Vucins

Viesturs Vucins can c more experience of run global super-carriers – phone operators with w wide reach and capacit than any other individu

A founder and for president of Unisource, strategic alliance betw the Dutch, Swiss, Spa and Swedish telecoms op tors, he has now b appointed president chief executive of Gl One, the strategic alli between Deutsche Telek France Télécom and Sp of the US.

FT announcement – 1996

Deutsche Bank – 2001

People

We introduce *Richard Madeley*, a Managing Director of JPMorgan Private Bank and a senior banker with responsibility for developing business within the UK

Looking back, I realize that mine is not the typical career path a private banker might embark on now! I started life as a Royal Marines Officer, serving in a variety of operational and peacetime roles for some 12 years. My City career began in the mid 1980s when I joined Mercury Asset Management. Here I had responsibility for marketing and client acquisition and developed extensive contacts with the UK's leading intermediary community. During this time I worked closely with leading UK tax and trust advisors and became a member of the Society of Trust and Estate Practitioners.

In the mid 1990s, I took on a management role at UBS where, following the merger with SBC, I was asked to develop their UK domestic business. It was a challenging and rewarding period and one which shaped my thinking about what clients need and how banks should respond. After a brief spell at Deutsche Bank in 2001, I decided to extend my management experience and set up a new business. Together with a former UBS colleague we defined, funded and established a specialist hedge fund risk management group. It was a hectic, stressful but very exciting time during which we all expanded our personal and professional horizons considerably. Ultimately the uncertain markets of 2003-2004 created a difficult legacy for the business and in early 2005 my co-founder and I decided to sell out our interests and go our separate ways.

In deciding to return to private banking I was immediately drawn to JPMorgan because of its culture, reputation and capabilities. In particular I wanted to ensure that in taking on a role as a banker, I would be able to devote adequate time to providing clients with the level of service that they need, rather than being swamped with relationships as in many other private banks. I was delighted that there was an opportunity to join Olivier de Givenchy's team and to be part of the team building the UK business for the bank.

I am married, live in London and Oxfordshire and have three school-aged children. In my spare time I enjoy skiing, golf, gardening and opera.

J.P. Morgan – 2005

David Rosier, chairman of Thurleigh Investment Managers and Richard Madeley, managing director and senior banker, JP Morgan Private Bank UK

With David Rosier, who originally hired me at MAM, at the 2011 PAM Awards

Meeting HRH Prince Philip at an SBSA reception in Buckingham Palace – 2012

NEW ASSISTANTS

Victoria Broackes is Senior Curator in the V&A Department of Theatre & Performance. She runs the annual London Design Festival at the V&A and has curated international touring exhibitions on David Bowie and Pink Floyd. Mother of four daughters (and daughter of former Prime Warden, Sir Nigel Broackes), she is a Trustee of Kids in Museums, Handel and Hendrix in London, adviser to the Holocaust Memorial Centre and alumni member of the Court of the Royal College of Art.

Cassandra Goad has been a jeweller and goldsmith all her working career, having been fascinated by jewellery since childhood. After an apprenticeship with Andrew Grima, she set up her jewellery business, Cassandra Goad, nearly 35 years ago. She is a trustee of St Mark's Foundation; a fellow of the Royal Society of Arts; and a member of the Chelsea Arts Club and of the Philanthropy Committee at C. Hoare and Co. She also works closely with a number of charities such as the Endeavour Fund personally and through her business.

Joanna Hardy is an independent fine jewellery specialist with more than 35 years of experience in the jewellery industry. She began her career training as a goldsmith at Sir John Cass College and became one of the first women to be a polished diamond dealer in Antwerp before joining Philips the Auctioneers in London. She was senior jewellery specialist and auctioneer at Sotheby's for 14 years and since 2009 has worked independently. Joanna lectures, curates and writes – both as a journalist specialising in jewellery and as an author of books. She is a Fellow of the Gemmological Association, Fellow of The Royal Society of Arts, a Trustee Board member of Gem-A and is a regular jewellery specialist on the BBC *Antiques Roadshow*.

Richard Madeley
After 30 years in private client wealth management, latterly as Managing Director at JP Morgan and Edmond de Rothschild, Richard Madeley now works independently, helping family investment offices raise and invest their capital. He began his City career in the 1980s after serving 12 years in the Royal Marines. Richard was educated at Eton College and beyond his commitment to the Goldsmiths' Company, is actively involved in Special Forces charities.

Election to the Court of the Worshipful Company of Goldsmiths – 2017

**Richard Madeley's Court Cup,
Clive Burr and Jane Short**

2019

925 sterling silver, silver-gilt, vitreous enamel

Madeley explains that he too wanted a cup that "captured a bit of my life story", thus he sketched it as a remembrance of his twelve years of service in the Royal Marines. The knop takes the form of a globe, enamelled in basse-taille to show the oceans with landmasses picked out in gold. Both the globe and the gilded wreaths are Marine emblems. The foot is engraved with waves referring to a life at sea, while the engraved mountains on the cup itself point to "my love of skiing and mountain life." The cup was spun by Clive Burr while the enamelling of the globe and the engraving of the mountain range is the work of Jane Short. Clive Burr subtly gilded the inside of the cup a pale gold, recalling Norwegian winter snowlight. Madeley comments: "Every time I use it, I am struck by its symmetry and style and it gives me enormous pleasure."

9

*My Court Cup. Traditionally commissioned for new
assistants of the company – 2019*

Off duty at a wedding in Palermo, Sicily – 2021

Chapter Eight

Reflections

Although I am probably only two thirds of the way through my life, the clear reality is that I have probably peaked in terms of life's accomplishments and it will be mostly 'downhill from here'. The only significant (expected) career event ahead is that of becoming the Prime Warden of the Goldsmiths' Company in about 2030, which will be a very special year for both Carol and me. Mostly, my time will be spent gradually winding down from advisory and fundraising work, although hopefully not breaking off entirely, and becoming more home-focused with gardening, golf and other family-centric activities becoming gradually more important. I am also determined to do some more travelling and visit some of the more far-flung and non-touristy parts of the world. It is, I suppose, the time of life when the baton passes to the younger generation and the balance of responsibility and the parent-child dynamic progressively reverses.

It gives me the right to reflect on my life a little and, without fear or favour, make some observations. I think the first important observation to make is to recognise how lucky I have been to have lived my life in freedom and peace, without any direct exposure to the real suffering that exists all around. By suffering, I don't just mean physical suffering, but the mental, financial, spiritual, emotional and other burdens that so many people carry with them through life. I was given a privileged start with a close and caring family and have found the love and support of a wonderful wife through my adult life. But there is more to it than that and I consider that I was fortunate to be born when I was, after the disruption of the world wars and before our national identity and traditions were undermined by the onset of globalised cultural and commercial ambitions, and the immediacy and instant gratification of digital media and communication. England in the 1960s – at least for me in our peaceful house in Margery Lane – was extraordinarily innocent and I could grow up at my own speed in a safe environment. Something of a rarity even then, I imagine, but almost unheard of now.

I don't harbour any regrets, although undoubtedly some things didn't play out quite as I expected. Mind you, I have always believed that the things that don't go to plan in life can often prove more useful as a learning process than all the things that go well. On that basis alone, I ought to be immeasurably wise by now! However, from time to time we all wonder 'what might have been' if we had made different choices, such as if I had stayed in the Royal Marines for a full career, for example. All I know is that I wouldn't have enjoyed the same stable family time that I have done. Possibly the nearest I have to a regret is not having gone to university from school and to build out a broader academic base for everything that life has thrown at me since. Of course, I didn't miss it at the time – indeed, I was only too glad to get stuck into the challenges of a career in the Royal Marines. But I secretly harbour a slight academic inferiority complex for not having challenged myself in this area as extensively as I have challenged myself in other areas. Be that as it may, I have pursued my life at full pace and still don't really know how to slow down and relax, something the children increasingly urge me to do. Perhaps this will be the biggest challenge of retirement, slowing down, either out of choice or out of necessity. I think the best answer is to find some new hobbies!

So perhaps it is time to draw up a bucket list of things I must do before senility finally sets in. Such a list might include the following:

- Motorcycling through Chile from the deserts to Patagonia – planned
- Surfing in Hawaii – although I need to learn first, probably in Cornwall
- Visiting Antarctica and walking on the icefields – planned
- Trekking in Alaska or northern Norway with dog sleds
- Diving on the Great Barrier Reef
- A High Altitude Low Opening (HALO) parachute jump
- A riding safari during the migration season
- Buying a boat and exploring some of Europe's riverways

The list is endless in my mind, but I suspect that not many are very high up Carol's wish list and I don't really want to have to do them all on my own. For some reason, she remains concerned about me being reckless (I can't think why) and disappearing without trace. The idea of buying a boat is certainly high up my list, but I think Carol is nervous that I will become some tyrannical Captain Bligh character and make her life a misery. I always thought that 'messing about on boats' was what all men eventually ended up doing.

Philosophising about life is seductive and cathartic, but inevitably we all end up sounding like Victor Meldrew in *One Foot in the Grave*, the 1990s sitcom character portraying an increasingly recalcitrant and misunderstood man facing up to change. Ironically, his was often the voice of sanity in an increasingly crazy escalation of events. Is this to be my destiny? Perhaps we all harbour some sense of personal disappointment that we didn't achieve more in life or wish we could relive certain special periods. I sense this is what sometimes drives otherwise sane and sensible married couples to part at this stage in their lives in search of something they feel is missing. In that respect, I feel immeasurably lucky.

So, what has life really taught me? Most importantly, it is to lead your own life and follow your instincts. Don't try and lead the life you think you ought to or the one you feel pressured to adopt; you only have one life to lead and you mustn't waste it. It is so easy to watch time slide by, waiting for the 'right' moment, only to miss something altogether. I find it reassuring how often our first impressions and first reactions prove correct and we can lose so much time agonising over irrelevancies. Opportunities occur all the time, but they aren't always obvious and need to be grabbed by the scruff of the neck and exploited. It is also important to have fun and I have never understood why fun is often seen as a frivolous or unprofessional word. It is incredibly important to have fun in life and generally the things we enjoy doing, we do better anyway. There are far too many serious people in the world already, weighed down by life's pressures, and so I think it is partly our duty to create happiness and enjoyment when we can… and not feel guilty about it.

The demon in all our lives can be money – the desire for it, the lack of it and undoubtedly the expectation of it. Yet money can so easily blind us to the more important things in life. The two truisms about money are that everyone assumes you are richer than you are, but that there is always someone else who is richer! I think the situation is inherently complicated by family wealth and how this might eventually flow down to the next generation. This wasn't an issue for me as my parents had used up almost all their savings by the time they died and there was a minimal distribution. In fact, if they had lived another five years, it could have been quite a problem. This, of course, is the dilemma in deciding when or how much to pass on to the next generation and it is very difficult to determine how much is needed to protect one's lifestyle in the absence of a salary and with an imprecise number of years to plan for. We are working through this sensitive balance at the moment, trying to balance our natural desire to assist the children with housing and their own children's costs, while ensuring that we don't build up problems for ourselves. We have already learned that to give the expectation of a distribution that then proves undeliverable is worse than saying nothing at all. On balance, our instinct is to be conservative about distributions for the time being and try and provide individual support as and when needed.

The irony is that while money creates choice in life, this doesn't always lead to better decisions, and we all know pampered but ultimately unhappy people. All too often, the quest for money can become a vicious spiral where working flat out leaves no time for pleasure and perversely creates the necessity of having to pay for help with the everyday chores. This can quickly develop into a 'reverse poverty trap' where one can't afford to step off the merry-go-round as the money keeps everything else afloat, when, in fact, a rethink on the important aspects of life, family and marriage could present different choices. So, my advice is to treasure the things that money can't buy: happiness, love, family and friends, job satisfaction and all the memories that go with these.

In a strange way, growing older is also a relief. You no longer have to thrust and jockey for the things that seem so important when you were younger, and you can relax in the knowledge that things will probably all work out in the end. Working with people you don't respect or that you simply dislike becomes a thing of the past and you can make genuine choices about how and with whom to spend your time. I am still getting used to this aspect as, for me, work has been part of what has defined me in many respects and so shaping my life without the discipline of a regular job is still new and somewhat strange, and I keep thinking that I should be working for a specific objective, when perhaps the objective is to relax and find new interests. This element of my life is still transitioning, but I do feel that a weight of urgency and responsibility has been lifted off me and most aspects of our life seem well set.

The one remaining big change to come will be the inevitable downsizing from Bottom Farm. The house itself is an ideal size to accommodate occasional visits by the family yet be manageable for just the two of us. The problem with Bottom Farm is also part of what makes it so special, namely the surroundings, the barns and the garden, all of which consume time, energy and, increasingly, money. My preference is to try and make it work and stay here until I am removed in a box, but I suspect that practicality and common sense will eventually prevail and we will find somewhere new. My preference is to be by water, either the sea (probably too far away) or a river. So we keep a weather eye on properties that might appeal, even though there is no urgent decision to be made.

And I guess this brings me up to date on where I find myself at the start of 2023, looking back over my life. It has been both cathartic and fun to revisit memories and tie together the journey of my life so far. I feel immeasurably healthier than when I started this story, as the doctors had been rather gloomy about the prognosis for my heart initially. I am certainly not ready to disappear and may live to regret the indiscretions and candour in some of my stories. If so, I apologise in advance. This book started off as simply a letter to the children, but has morphed into rather more. But, darling children, I am above all so proud of each one of you, of what you have already achieved in your lives and the choices you have made. If any of these reflections act as a cautionary tale, then take heed, but I hope you will simply recognise my desire to do my duty, to make my life worthwhile in some way and to have fun along the way. Follow your own hearts and lead your lives as fully as I think I have lived mine, and you won't have any regrets.

Postscript

Regrettably, following the submission of this script to the publishers, I was diagnosed and operated on in late 2023 for a brain tumour which has rather eclipsed the more minor heart issues I was facing before. While the standard prognosis for this particular cancer is not promising, I remain very positive and determined to live whatever life I may have left, to the full.

Interestingly, as I reflect on my changing circumstances, I realise that I do not have any fear of death itself, simply the disappointment that I will miss the landmark moments with family and friends to celebrate career successes, children and other major events in their lives. I may also miss the opportunity to tick off many of the holidays and exploits that I had to set myself to achieve in my lifetime. Perhaps Carol can tick a few more off for me!

In the meantime I will remain a stubborn and reluctant patient, determined to prove my resilience and contempt for statistical outcomes.